Ultramarathon

James E. Shapiro

ECHO POINT BOOKS & MEDIA, LLC
Brattleboro, Vermont

Published by Echo Point Books & Media
Brattleboro, Vermont
www.EchoPointBooks.com

Copyright © 1980, 2021 by Jim Shapiro
Photographs copyright © 1980, 2021 by Joe Greene

Ultramarathon
ISBN: 978-1-64837-074-8 (casebound)
       978-1-64837-075-5 (paperback)

Interior design by Cathy Marinaccio

Cover design by Kaitlyn Whitaker

Cover image: *Running toward the Fitz Roy mountain in Pantogonia,
Argentina,* by Andrea Leopardi (@whatyouhide),
courtesy of unsplash

To my sister, Harriet

Acknowledgments

Any book depends on many other people. A complete list of thanks for this one would be very long indeed. Everyone mentioned or quoted in the book was, without exception, generous and patient with intrusive questions.

In this country I would particularly like to thank Ted Corbitt, Richard Innamorato and Max and Jenny White. In France I benefited from the splendid hospitality of Michel and Jacqueline Carcenac and Elias and Molly Magaram. In England, Mr. and Mrs. John Jewell were especially patient with my endless demands. I very much appreciate the hospitality there of Don Ritchie and Mr. and Mrs. Alec Ritchie; also, Mr. and Mrs. Bernard Gomersall and Carol and Cavin Woodward. During my South African visit Tony and Janet Sherrard were delightful hosts. For their help and orientation thanks are due to Len and Joyce Keating, Mr. and Mrs. Jackie Mekler, Mick Winn, Derek Palframan, Adrian Alexander, Mike Toms, Vernon Jones, Fred Morrison, Wally Hayward and Mavis Hutchison.

For their boost over the thorny hedge of statistics special mention goes to Andy Milroy, Peter Lovesey and particularly Nick Marshall.

And for their help in making the process of producing the book so smooth and pleasant thanks go to Peter Ginsberg and my editor, Susan Rosen.

To Go On.

When Everything Else

Wants To Stop . . .

It is not pain I feel but sinking.
My involvement with the world grows dimmer.
It occurs to me that it would be nice to keel over.
A barely audible whisper says it would be a way out.
It seems almost impossible to bother any more . . .
but I do.

Ultramarathon

Contents

"The runner does not know how or why he runs. He only knows that he must run, and in so doing he expresses himself as he can in no other way. He creates out of instability and conflict something that gives pleasure to himself and others, because it releases feelings of beauty and power latent within us all."

Roger Bannister, *The Four Minute Mile*

Roger Colahan takes the pedestrian route
over the Hudson River's Bear Mountain Bridge.

1.
THE LONGEST RUN OF MY LIFE

Early this morning, when I awoke (after one of the more troubled sleeps I've had), the English weather was cold and gray. My splitting headache didn't leave me until I carried my gear onto the sun-bathed running track at the Crystal Palace Sports Centre in south London, the site of Britain's major track meets. Only then did the experience seem real. The afternoon of the twenty-seventh day of October, 1979, had finally arrived.

I felt remarkably calm for someone about to set off on a 24-hour run around and around a 400-meter track in the company of some other lunatics, in an attempt to see how many miles we could cram into our allotted time. But at the very last, after waiting a year for a single day's appearance, it seemed better to get on with it rather than speculate one instant longer.

For purposes of record-keeping and simplicity, twenty-four-hour races are always held on a track. Runners in the terminal stages of exhaustion would be a hazard on public roadways. Even navigating the straight lines and double set of curves on a running track can become a strenuous business for those able to endure the last full measure of one of ultramarathoning's longest trials. In a 24-hour run, only a few will finish without walking a portion. Properly done, such a trial can take one out to the edge of human endurance.

I shook hands with a few runners I knew. A few others introduced themselves, including Joe Record of Australia and Jan Knippenberg of the Netherlands. For the rest, there will be time enough to make their acquaintance. Under prolonged stress we may well prove unwittingly interesting to each other, but all that is yet to come . . .

There are 17 of us lined up; everyone is quiet. All of us were invited by a special subcommittee of the English Roadrunner's Club, with the proviso that we thought ourselves capable of covering a minimum of 130 miles. What novice to the race could claim that without pause? During 24 hours, a thousand things can go wrong.

3

A starter raises his arm. Dark shapes at the sides of the track remind me of the tiny cluster of spectators and handlers gathered to watch. I wonder if they will not be quite sick of observing us by the next afternoon. The gun fires. After months of training, anxiety, swings between hopefulness and apprehension, I am in motion at last. It feels, of course, completely normal and unremarkable.

As we round the first curve we are all in a bunch except for Don Ritchie, a Scot, who storms into the lead in his customary style. Within two hundred meters he has opened up quite a lot of daylight but he is, after all, world record holder for a lot of distances, including 100 miles, and he is entitled to try it the way he thinks best. (Less than a week earlier he was in the States running the New York City Marathon. He then returned to his home in the northern end of Scotland before taking a second-class train trip to London for this labor. But then Peter Hart, a rosy-cheeked farmer who is also in the race, was out digging potatoes on his farm till three in the afternoon yesterday, when the rains forced him to stop. I feel as though I've been pampering myself, lying around a hotel room for a week.)

Since Ritchie sets a pace of 5 minutes and 44 seconds per mile, as the rest of us are running 7:30 to 8:30, he streaks by every few laps. Every time someone passes me, I wonder whether I should move into the second lane. But mixed in with genuine goodwill toward my fellow competitors is a measure of prickliness. Let them go around me, I mulishly decide.

As spectators watch us near the starting line, they snap pictures. My sister, Harriet, is among them with some English friends of ours, and every two minutes, as I flit past, I grin inanely. I can't help it. Harriet told me before the start that I looked radiant and I know I am buzzing along with the needle jammed up on a full tank. This delight can't last but it's legitimate to be goofy for a bit. Since we started at four o'clock the bright sun on this clear cloudless afternoon begins to fall perceptibly toward the edge of the roof which overhangs the stadium seats. Although the sky is wide and open overhead, and trees and grass can be glimpsed at one end of this complex, there is nothing especially interesting to look at.

Earlier in the week, I have come down twice to run a little and soak up a feeling for the place. On an empty gray day with the blank floodlights and distant television towers piercing the drizzle, the place resembled nothing so much as a sterile astronaut training center. The rattle of a beer can driven by the wind carried from one far end of the stadium to the other. At least with all of us here the place and the enterprise have an element of cheer. From the nearby zoo I hear the witless braying of a lonely donkey. The sun dips further and the tiny faces of the recorders in the press box dwindle into obscurity.

One man or woman is assigned to each of us to do nothing but chart our progress through time and space with the aid of a scoring card. Each single revolution we make is recorded and timed down to the second. We are playing for keeps, knocking ourselves out for the sake of numbers and lists that only we and a few dozen others around the world will bother to read and remember.

What do I think about in these early stages, when a mere 22 to 23 hours loom ahead? What ennobling declarations of will do I review in my mind? Not many. To an outsider, it may perhaps seem that one would surely go mad with boredom or anxiety, running around like a lab animal on a treadmill. I admit to sometimes having such fears myself. I am a road runner. I love mucking through the streets of my hometown of Manhattan, or scooting out the door with a small day pack heading due north with a pal or two, for whatever faraway train station we have decided to get to that Sunday. We do this to experience the whole joy of being on the road, moving from one fixed point to another with the goal of finishing steadily drawing nearer all the while, as we climb and descend in a sometimes easy harmony with the hills and the rotaries and the shoulders of countless roadways that meander through the world. Something always happens; there is a bit of fullness at the end of such a day—nothing of stunning spiritual dimensions but deeply pleasurable all the same. There are worse hobbies.

This time I have been foolish enough to enlist in something that I know very little about, running in a confined space. I am running now against the clock. There is no set distance to get through today. It is whatever maximum flesh and spirit can bear. Anything less will be a failure. This is no 30-mile jaunt—I will push on hopefully 4 to 5 times longer than that. I have tried running on tracks. A few times this year I have run around the reservoir in Central Park, a 1½-mile cinder loop, some 22 times. But the idea of 80 circuits on a ¼-mile track was sufficient to cool any notion of doing it frequently. A last attempt to cover 20-odd miles on a track a few weeks before leaving for England was an experience that set my mental teeth on edge. One more doubt to conjure with in private moments as I wondered if I was getting myself into a stress test whose rules I would find I detested. It was then still possible to beg off and go run the Millau-to-Belvès 257-kilometer road race in southern France which my friend, Michel Carcenac, was putting on. That race, after all, was a lovely point-to-point bit of madness through the beautiful Dordogne valley.

But the 24-hour is one of the classics. Too many men and women I admired had done it and I hadn't. It had too perfect a shape and handle for me not to yearn to pick it up and use it to pry myself open to see what I am made of. One learns to accept the little destinies one creates for oneself. Besides, a race would be impossibly dull without some fear and doubt to wrestle against.

In this first hour or two all seems well. If anything, I am going a touch faster than I really want. It is easy to dip below 8 minutes a mile but that is too fast. I look at a digital clock with red numerals every time I pass the starting line. As I approach the clock, tiny things interest me. First, I notice that it is powered by car batteries, covered with thick plastic by some helpful soul in case unexpected rain descends. This took several laps to perceive. Soon I begin to wonder where I should avert my eyes to carry the memory of the time around with me so that I can calculate my per-lap time. A single stride forward or back changes my angle of vision on the sign and makes a difference of a second or two in what my elapsed time will be.

Such minutiae are replaced by other minor events on the track. The race officials are busy with their steel tape and red flags, measuring the inner curb in order to determine to the inch where we will pass 100 miles. They can afford to look that far ahead; I can't. I begin to lose interest in my lap times. I am running in what feels like easy neutral gear, just doing it, letting myself run, trying to stay as easy as I can.

I hang behind a few knots of people, content not to talk, preferring to feel whatever it is I am feeling. I feel pleasantly detached and, for the moment, socially self-sufficient. Race chatter drags me down very quickly, so I save a few comments for my two handlers, Melanie Marcus and Joe Greene. Melanie has got our little site perked up with a stove, a brightly colored tent, a suitcase with my extra clothing and doodads, and stacks of food and drinks. It is nice to have friends take care of you, nice not to have to worry. My business is to save every bit of energy for running. They have the drab end of the operation, but as a team we understand each other.

I notice the other tents as I go by. There are big ones and little ones. The Finns have a tent. The Peddie family has another. The refreshment stewards who service us have one, too. Jack Bristol, a hardy type and the other American in the race, has slung his backpack near our site and runs on in contentedly, independent style.

Jack and I have shared some stretches of American roadway before in other long races but he is going much faster than I am, so during the first few hours we have limited social contact. He says such things as "Huffa-puff!" when he glides by, lapping me over and over. I say "Yes, sir!" a phrase I've absorbed from a running pal in New York. Then Jack goes around again, saying "Huffa-puff!" with the same easy relish. It is already slightly mad and I wonder if our exchange will become unbearable after several hundred repetitions (it never does). It's funny. Although we are all trying to run each other's guts out, we enjoy each other's company and chat at odd intervals like straphangers on the subway.

Darkness comes early. I am doing between 6¾ to 7 miles an hour. I feel pleased at banging along so steadily and only mildly grim when the huge electronic scoreboard at one end lights up with our positions and distance covered. Out of our field of 17 I am running for a while in the next to last slot, but I had expected that. My strategy is simple. The world record is officially 161 miles, 545 yards. If I can, I will try to surpass it. I had looked into the mirror a few times the last day or so to see how rested I was, to see who was staring back. Was I a loon or a dark horse? I couldn't be sure so I decided to play a razor's edge.

I would run steadily, even-paced, with minimal slowdown. Let the speed boys run themselves out. I figured that the natural focus point for most people would be 100 miles and then their psychological resistance would weaken. Very well. I would nurse myself along to 100 as easily as I could and then put the pressure on by remaining steady. I would stay aloof from dueling for position on the track. The trick was to run your own best possible race and hope that such strategy brought you out on top. If not, well then probably nothing would have done so, certainly not an injudicious squandering of your resources. Spill your limited energy too recklessly early on and the closing hours would be brutal.

Go easy. Go relaxed. Save energy. Ignore the world. Forget the deep habit of every runner who loves to race which makes you yearn to close up on the pair of heels in front. The 24-hour is a special monster. It required, I felt, obedience to special laws or it would flatten the runner as indifferently as a hippo flopping down on a blade of grass.

7

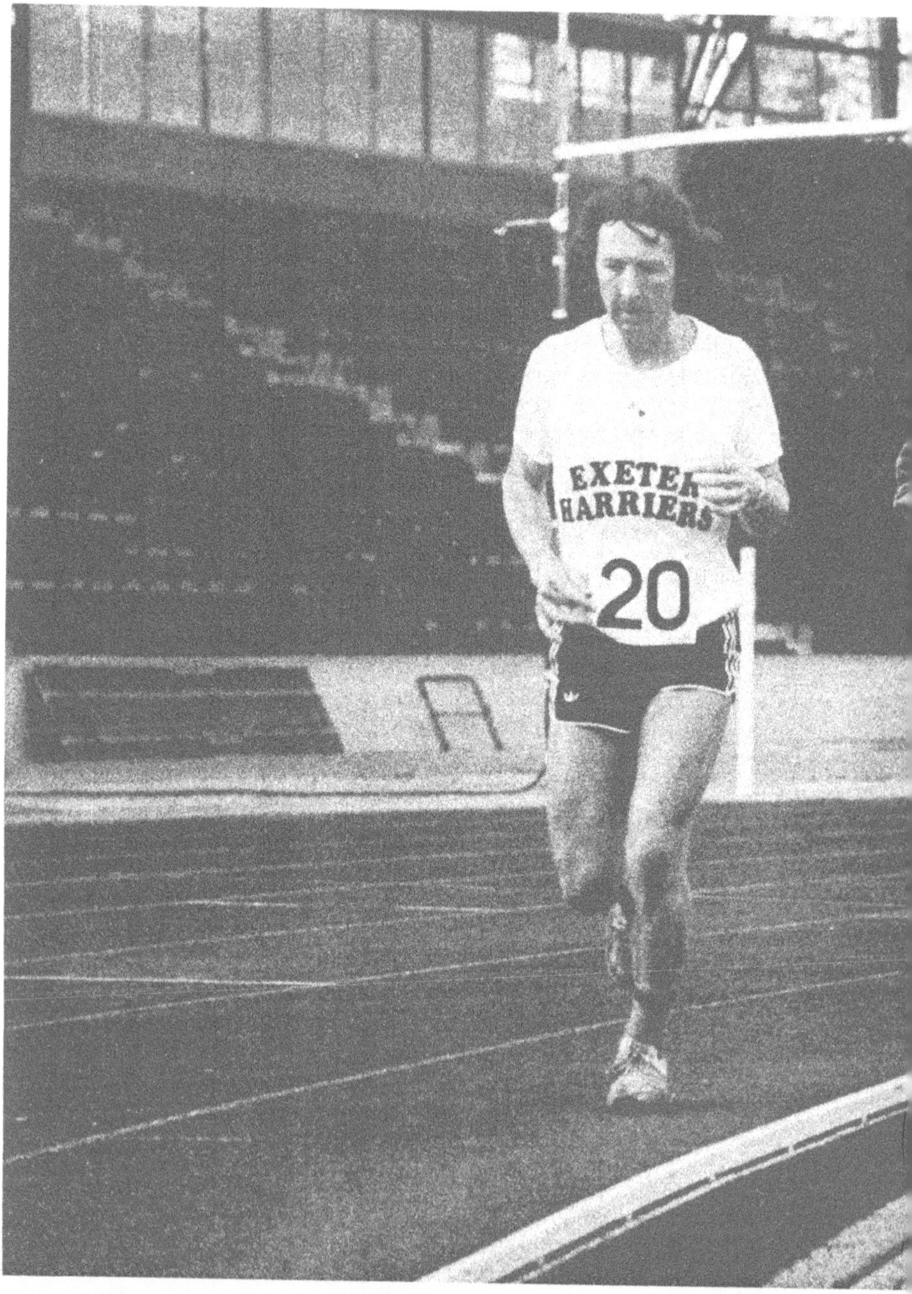
EXETER
HARRIERS
20

Those were the rules I had smoked out in my own private cave and studied over and over on long runs up the Hudson River, rehearsing through the seven or eight hours of pounding: "This is what the last eight will be like in London. Legs dying but keep the swing going. Keep going, you bastard, just easy now. Just get me to the Putnam County line and then you can rest." And then, when I had done that, I would ask a little more. And I would get up on days when my body was jaded and just do it, drawing out of the deep, dark area that forces one to act, because if I ever stopped to analyze in the wrong way I would never do it.

You cannot think your way through training. You can only do it. Nor can you worry too much about anything other than present space. I had found that out in March when I did a 24-hour training run. In the latter stages, when the end seemed impossibly far off, I had to chide my nagging analytical side for trying to think about the miles left to travel. It was enough just to worry about what I was doing right then. And there is sometimes that inevitable desire to just lie down and say, well, I will continue when it gets easier, but such longings cannot be given into. You get it done by doing it.

Nothing simpler to say—and not even so hard to do—*if* you just do it. Intellect does not propel one along in perpetual motion— something else you find room for does that. So after all my internal yakking and easy breathing and out-loud muttering during the solitude of long runs, I am not surprised to be behind. But all the same, I think: Just wait, you bastards. The scoreboard can't accommodate all our names and the laggards like myself have to wait before we can deserve to appear. So as the floodlights light up our little underworld empire, I bide my time and run on.

At about three hours, there is a problem. I have managed until now to ignore its faint warning signals but the problem is clearly not going away easily. In spite of the advice of friends to train as much as possible around a track, I didn't do much of it. Now my right leg, unaccustomed to pushing (we are running with our left sides facing the inside of the track), begins to develop an acorn-sized throb on the inside of the upper thigh. In terms of relative discomfort it is nothing, but it casts a long shadow. It threatens the one thing I have most feared—not immense fatigue but a sudden giving out of muscle or tendon, something irremediable, some unforeseen hairline crack of vulnerability that will split the whole enterprise down the middle.

Part of my program is to stop every hour and fifty-five minutes and do five minutes of stretching on a foam rubber mat spread out on the grass. By eight in the evening it is chilly and when I lay down on the mat it is wet with condensation. Steam swirls off from my sweatsuit. I work my thighs as best as I can to help them out. I know my old friends are in trouble. But they are sullen and deceptive and when I stand up I think I am all right again. It is only when I start running once more that I feel the right cramp begin to latch in to where it has hammered its crampon, and the left begins to mirror the pain as well.

For a while, this is all I think about. Perhaps it has nothing to do with my right leg pushing harder. Perhaps, I think, I am just going to get screwed out here. I have never had my thighs cramp so ridiculously early. Then I remember that everyone who does these things runs through problems that seem horrendous and then fade. Sometimes things just go away. And it is the fear of not knowing the ultimate effect that is worst, not the thing itself. I feel more cheerful.

The miles click by. What was this fantasy about a nightmare of monotony? The hours do not quite recede effortlessly, especially when the face of the red digital speaks so bluntly at every turn, but there is a certain pleasure in going around and around the little village. There is the knowledge that high up in the press box one's achievement is being meticulously collated. There are the drinks to enjoy every couple of laps. I squeeze the little bottle, swallow the squirt, catch my breath, repeat and suddenly the lap is gone. Flip the bottle back to Melanie.

Knippenberg, the Dutchman whose thin frame with the bony elbows has puttered past me with monotonous regularity, begins to have time now to relax. We get to know each other in an attenuated sort of way. There is just time for one exchange on every encounter. As he runs ahead out of earshot I call out a last reply. Then we pick it up again later on. Ritchie shoots past and asks how I'm doing. Startled that he has broken his long silence, I tell him I'm fine.

The tartan surface, a rubberized asphalt, is an orangey-brown kind of color, and the inside lane, marked—as all the lanes are—by white stripes, is worn a bit scant on the main footpath which thousands of runners have covered before us. Sadly anonymous the world, hard to find the spirit of past races on this particular track. From the loudspeaker occasionally emerges an announcer's voice, with a British accent, commenting on the status of the race. For a long while now Ritchie has appeared to be on course for a new 100-mile record—if he can keep it up. The rest of us urge him on a little bit and he also gets plugs from people

11

watching. My sister comes to the edge of the track, a face in the window of my cell, and says she'll be returning to London. Next lap we say good night. I hope that when she returns tomorrow morning she will find me still running. It is another long plumb line I wire myself to, very thin, based on the improbabilities and hazards of many hours ahead but through all this easy shuffling I call running I am still optimistic.

My sister vanishes and I consider for a moment that she will actually go to sleep in a warm bed far away in central London, wake up on another day, have breakfast, and all the while I will be awake, still here. It simply is not real. But if this isn't real, I couldn't imagine what is. I go back to my work. Perhaps I do not really think very much. Things come in and then go out again. However long the race may now seem to be, it will end somehow.

At 7:45 P.M. it is 4¾ hours into the race since clocks are set back an hour tonight. The race will end at 3:00 tomorrow. My thighs are worse. I do some quick stretching but that doesn't help. First food of the evening is chicken soup. The body expends about 100 calories a mile, 700 calories an hour, perhaps 16,000 calories by the end of the race. There is no way to eat fast enough, but fat metabolism will carry one in large measure for the whole distance. I spent two days in local supermarkets looking for instant foods that seemed nutritional. The chicken soup is delicious but when I try to eat a banana it tastes repugnant.

Clothing is an intermittent concern. Some men are running barelegged; others like myself have changed into long-sleeved tops and bottoms. It takes me a long time to decide to change from a net T-shirt and shorts, even though I can see Melanie bundling up during the early evening. There is always the chance of losing too much body heat, so I call out on one lap for her to pin numbers on such-and-such a sweatsuit. When the clothing will be ready occupies a couple of laps. Then another lap or two before I stop and another mile is gone. So they go, still seeping away with minimal effort, punctuated by little events which are most important to this self-involving venture.

For example, there is the critical matter of pissing. There is no toilet by the side of the track so we must run into one of the dressing rooms under the stands. The rules ask us to come back on the track exactly where we left off, but no one is checking to see that we do so. The mere idea of cheating among such a group seems an absurdity that I do not even conjure with. All the same I watch myself and note a conveniently painted bar which I use to mark my departure, so as to run at an angle to the dressing room door with minimal wastage of meters. What a waste, I think, sorry to lose a minute or so.

But a little later in the evening I see two runners having a harmonious pee side by side on the grassy shoulder that meanders off toward a fence. There are no women in the race, and those who are handlers do not wander down here. I decide: I, too, will use this corner. I am drinking heavily on such a cool night although the obvious escapes me. I assume that tension, or excitement, or the weather is making me urinate sometimes as frequently as every six or seven laps.

I keep thinking how I need to drink to get at least a few calories from the fruit juices and the special mix I've asked my handlers to put in my drinks. Among other things, it consists of dried banana, ground seashells and sesame seeds. Plus I do feel mildly dizzy and wobbly when I stop, so I figure: drink more. These stops interrupt the rhythm of the running. And this reminds me a little sadly that it has yet to feel like a long solo run which unfolds in stages, when each stop only breaks the spell. Distractions tug at me. The red digital cuts into my attention every two minutes and few seconds when I run past it. And then a full bladder says, "Notice me." I say, "Wait." The pressure subsides and then, a hundred meters later, says, "Good God, what are you waiting for? I'm not getting any better." "But you're being childish," I answer. "Very well, feel this now," comes a sullen answer and as the precious peeing corner hoves into view it seems impossible to hold off another lap. I give in to the inevitable, although I have to admit how lovely a good piss feels—even though the steaming jet of water seems a bit of a distant phantom.

When I stop, the quality of attention I have standing there is the same one gets when stepping down momentarily from a train onto a railway platform after hours of travel. My body receptors are still vibrating with movement. Cessation of motion is a mere blink. Only the sweep that carries one forward can be real just then. So I hitch up my long sweats and before rejoining the invisible groove I glance back to ascertain the present traffic conditions.

Around this time, about five hours into it, Ritchie's feet are slapping at a tremendous rate and I wonder how anyone can run pounding that hard for another 19 hours. Going by me, he says something I can't hear. "What's that?" I ask. "Damn silly race," he says now on my shoulder in the passing lane. It seems a bad attitude to have so early and I figure that he might drop out. I feel more certain of this later when he sits down on the track, a

13

blanket over his shoulders, while an attendant bandages his right foot to prevent a deep blister from getting worse. I hope in an impersonal way that he will soon fade back or drop out. I like Don very much, but I want to be the top survivor by the end of tomorrow's daylight.

The night wears on. A white mist dims the eerie sharpness of the floodlights. A few minutes after every hour I have Joe climb up to the official's box to check my progress. It is another focus point. Word is good till now: 1 hour—7¼ miles; 2 hours—14 miles; 3 hours—20¾ miles; 4 hours—27½ miles; 5 hours—34 miles; 6 hours—41 miles; 7 hours—47¼ miles.

After over 50 miles of running, Ritchie has dropped out. I think to myself that at least I will not be the first. Stalwart Mike Newton, running in shorts the entire time, is still making good time; he has moved into second place behind Bristol. The two of them go through 50 miles in less than 6½ hours, world record pace for 24 hours by a big margin. I figure they have to fade, but I shrug. Can't worry too much about them—I have some serious catching up to do, especially if they hold on reasonably well. Knippenberg has lost his social chatter, although most talk died out after about three hours. People are working now. Knippenberg complains when I ask him about stomach cramps. He mentions a race he ran not long ago which took him 40-odd hours to complete. Veterans of such efforts are not to be dismissed, so—although I remind myself of a sour and impoverished character in Balzac waiting for his relatives to die off—I cast a quick look at him. He just may not last, I think optimistically.

Once in a while now I pass someone else on a lap. This feels good. There are overheard bits of conversation. Frank Thomas, an Englishman, fills time a little by discussing 100-mile runs he has done over the moors and the fells of rural England. He runs lightly with an incredibly upright, springy carriage, but he is running conservatively. I josh him about his knit cap and what an atrocious color it is, but as we approach the midnight hours he grows quiet so I leave him alone. Enough is enough.

At ten o'clock John Jewell announces over the loudspeakers that there will be no more amplified comments until seven the following morning, so that local residents will not be disturbed. After he signs off, the message board, which spells out its words in yellow electric-light bulbs, posts information on our relative positions and times covered. Phoned-in or delivered messages are put on the board: So-and-so is thinking of you now with all her love—things like that. The silence of the stadium grows steadily deeper.

The runners wrestle with shoes that pinch. Now even the leaders begin to stop sometimes to grab a drink and walk a few yards. Extra pullovers are put on. The blue flames of camp stoves keep pots of tea on the boil, the steam rising from spigots straight up into the calm, unbroken cold. Off to the north the lights of central London brush the clouds with red. A dog howls somewhere nearby, but the donkey has been silent for hours. I am running on, still running, having gotten somewhere, going somewhere, all plans and shapes and shadows unsure, nothing to be distinguished from anything else because we are all still building, still falling, and it is too early yet to tell just who will finally rise and who will finally fall.

I don't mind running in circles. It turns out that I hardly notice the repetition, although I barely notice not noticing. I simply go on, trying to keep arm action relaxed, palms relaxed, release through my heels as my stretch teacher back home in New York instructed me. There is no boredom for me right now. I am used to night running. I think briefly of running home from a nighttime cooking job in Brooklyn, over the Brooklyn Bridge and up through the stone arroyos of lower Manhattan. That was lonely in the same nice way. Night running is always quieter and more detached.

At one in the morning, nine hours into the race, I really begin to suffer. Perhaps after the initial excitement has worn off and I discover how overly keyed up I must have been, I am paying the price. I cannot get comfortable with my legs, particularly my thighs. They have begun to really jam up now. There is real bite every time I stride. I make a last attempt to stretch. But now, when I get up from the Yoga mat and start off, I'm a victim of what I call "flash freeze," when after stopping the running your muscles almost immediately give in to severe tightening. I hobble along until I can get into the swing again.

Now what do I do? Plans are a bit shattered. Fifteen hours to go and I have gotten fucked. Most likely, I decide, it will get worse. Anything less than 130 miles will be a bitter disappointment. I know that. I have prepared myself a number of times for running much less even, but when it comes to considering it a likely possibility I feel wretched. A vast depression engulfs me. I could cry with frustration and weariness.

There is a bit of hurry, a bit of panic in the mixed-up mumble of my mind. All I have to do is turn my eyes slightly to one side and I can see the desire to drop out. I keep my gaze averted but all the same I feel awfully lonely. But I am not about to discuss it with Melanie or Joe or anyone else. I am in one of the worst hours

15

of running I have ever endured. In some odd way I am losing my nerve. But my memory comes to my aid and I remember other times. These things happen, and you get through them after a while. Bad patches don't go on forever.

This hour passes and other things happen. The horror fades and I notice an unusual problem for myself—blisters. These are the result of a mild spell of arrogance when I decided not to put Vaseline on my toes; my feet were tough enough already, I told myself that morning. Now I sit down on a chair and pull off a·shoe and a sock. I wince from the smell. Sure enough I find a blister the size of a grape between two toes. I tear at it to break the liquid and Vaseline the toes.

Meanwhile my friends on the track are not slowing down for my sake. I catch their glances as I sit. I know they are thinking about the yards they are gaining on me. I change my socks, retie my shoes, jump up and go at it again. My number in front is held on with four safety pins, which pass through metal eyelets stamped into the cardboard. The weight of the paper number makes it bounce with an audible tit-tot kind of noise. When I notice the sound, it seems detestable but hardly worth fussing over. I wonder now when I will no longer hear it again but that is like trying to watch at what point you fall asleep. The tit-tot grows even louder but by the end of the lap my mind is a pleasant heap of dry sand. I am running, he is running, we are all running.

Mike Newton runs past again for the umpteenth time. He certainly deserves credit for boldness for he has closed on Bristol and taken first place. Five days earlier we had met at Crystal Palace for a trial spin around the track. Mike complained of a sharp pain every time he flexed his right foot, just where foot and leg meet in front. "It's a sickening sort of pain," he said sadly, "the kind you feel when you bang your elbow. I couldn't run London-to-Brighton last month. My training's been way off now for weeks. So I thought today I'd just run easily for a while to test it out." I suggested he go easy the rest of the week, but then Mike looked even more pained. "Perhaps I better not even start the race," he said. "The thing is I've promised to run, I've put my name down. I don't know what to do. Maybe I'll just go ahead and do what I can for as long as I can. But I don't have the mental edge anymore. I've lost my enthusiasm." For someone trying out a sore foot, he moved along at a fair clip that day. I merely shook my head at a species of stubbornness I knew all too well, and went to lay down in the sun. Sunshine in England is too precious to waste, and I was forcing myself to cut back on training. It's easy to tell others to rest, but like all the compulsives I know who are involved in these madcap ventures, I decided that more rather than less is usually the easiest course to follow.

Tonight Mike is running with an easy clip-clop style, not going full tilt but all the same eating up the miles at an impressive pace. If he keeps it up, he could well get the world's record. Since he is too far ahead to worry about, I can afford to be nice. "You're going well," I tell him frequently. He shakes his head and mutters darkly about not lasting much longer, but he shows no external signs of wear.

Jack Bristol is slowing down as he nears 90 miles, and I begin to get back a lap sometimes. All the same his running style—the most graceful and flowing on the track—might carry him out of my reach all the way through. His habit is to start very hard, and then hang on. (He ran the Brighton race in England a few weeks earlier and was, I heard, first man over Westminster Bridge, clipping along at the start of a 55-mile plus race at sub-6 miling. He may have faded but he still took ninth place.)

At 1:00 a.m. I have gone 66 miles, and an hour later I am at 72 miles. I consider the numbers; at least if I drop out here I will have had a fairly decent workout. I imagine I am on my March run between my upper West Side apartment and my father's house 105 miles away in Dutchess County. I have clicked off the familiar Hudson River valley towns. Croton-on-Harmon (31 miles); Peekskill, where the steep and forested hills rise straight out of the water (40 miles); the Dutchess County signpost on the right-hand side of the road (50-odd miles) and now the city limits of Poughkeepsie (73 miles). In two more hours I will go through Staatsburg and Hyde Park before reaching the stoplight in Rhinebeck, New York, where I make a right-hand turn. Two hours to Rhinebeck. I think I can manage that. I am not swinging along now, but the worst of my apprehensions are beginning to quickly recede. My thighs are suffering but stable. I can live with that. There will be no grand surges tonight. No triumphant march through the distant barriers of a world record. I smile, abandoning that notion. I can make myself content with steadiness.

Three in the morning brings news of 78 miles, 200 yards behind me, which is the approximate range I had aimed for in my plans. When the lights go up on the board, I am in the top half of the field for the first time. Newton, still in first, is at 92 miles, 400 yards. Bristol is at 89 miles, 400 yards and Jones, an Englishman, is at 82 miles, 850 yards.

The signboard tells us that we are at the halfway point, twelve hours gone. The rest is downhill, it assures us, and my softening imagination gazes for a while at an immense imaginary plain which tips down toward the edge of the sky as if we were literally running now on a slight incline. This is not such an absurdity as it may sound. "Only twelve hours remain." It does mean something. And I am getting eager again. There is a pack of three or four men just a few minutes off and I give in for a while to the urge to chase. More frequently now, I begin to gain back a lap. I do my math and realize that to gain even a few miles on someone running strongly is very hard indeed. I am running miles that tick off between an 8:30 and an 8:50 pace.

The feline fog of Carl Sandburg finally makes its long delayed appearance. Beyond the sharp white light of our circle the city has grown steadily more silent and remote. A radio by the side of the track provides music from past and present. It adds a bit of cheerful color and absurdity to catch Elvis and Anita Ward and Stevie Wonder on each lap. One of the runners has gone off into deep space with earphones and some sort of radio hookup he has strapped around himself. Normally such devices elicit a snarl from me, but I am feeling charitable tonight and I go by without passing judgment.

Then, at 4:00 a.m., the radio falls silent except for a long siege of crackle. On the next lap I hear crackle again and it nettles my patience. There is no one around to turn it off. Such stress keeps shaving down the fine outer layers. The fog has settled in now with a vengeance. On the far side of the track, the figures turn dim, ghostly, and the atmosphere grows steadily smokier. Reports come down from the officials' box that they are having trouble reading our numbers.

We are all Jonahs, toppling down into the maw of weather that we ourselves seem to have created, as if the mental horizons I and my fellow travelers are padding across have become a dream both inside and out. Consider the fact that we are all going to be dead someday, and not a one of us here will be able to testify any longer to what this was like—not sad to think such a thought, just strange, odd. We certainly act alive, although the scene begins to resemble what I have read of forced marches, pilgrimages in northeast Brazil, the retreats of defeated troops. Strong men now begin to walk, plodding onward as if they had somewhere to go.

I see Newton talking to someone by the side of the track, and then he vanishes inside a tent. Word filters in a whisper through our little community: He is out now at 104 miles, 1,197 yards, and I feel a small wave of sorrow for him. At least he got a great

18

100-mile time from it, 13:09:15. That puts Jack into first place.

I have long since abandoned the idea of stopping for stretches, and I contemplate the ironic fact that it is far more comfortable to run for 24 hours than to try to ease through it. As long as I keep moving I will avoid freezing up, but my progress slows between four and five in the morning when I cover only six miles. I think of a few running friends in New York. It is midnight there and they have probably thought once or twice, gee, Jim's well into it now. I get a small smile out of that.

At five in the morning I have done 90¼, miles, and I tell Joe that I can smell 100 miles coming up. It is only a temporary goal. Too many 24-hour men strain to reach that and then crack shortly after, slumping, even the champions, from 8-minute to 11-minute miling. So I allow my enthusiasm a short leash. Someone tells me my pace will bring me out for 156 miles at the finish. I am slipping, not badly, but going down. There is no point in discussing the slowly rising waters. Like hemlock drinkers I can feel the numbness coming up, the slowly piercing message on a deeper level of fatigue that the muscles and tendons and bones are voiding even extraordinary stores. I get it most clearly in my feet, some sort of a raw feeling, as if they're long strips of flapping flesh. Oh, well, no point in backing off, I think, not even considering that idea anymore. I had made up my mind that everything would get consumed in the effort. I had made a pretense of saying that I would stop short of really damaging myself but that isn't true, and I have a brief moment just before dawn where I just nod at the realization. Okay, I think, we're just going on now.

"How are you doing?" Melanie asks. "Very comfortable," I say. "Well, not *too* comfortable."

I begin to weary of the night. All nights are the same, for in the last fierce hour before blue bleeds into black the cold deepens. The fog is thick and heavy and faces are recognizable only a few yards away. Peddie is releasing tremendous belches from his gnomelike frame. I kid him but he doesn't hear me. A moment later his belch reverberates through the entire stadium. From the nearby zoo a cock begins crowing, although there is little sign of day. Maybe, I think, in a try at humor, no one informed him of daylight savings time.

At six in the morning I complete 95¾ miles. About an hour and a quarter earlier, Bristol, still the leader, went through his 100-mile mark in 13:46:12. He is perhaps 9 miles, or about 36 laps, ahead. With 9 hours to go I must make up at least 4 laps every hour. It doesn't look likely. At 15:45:00 I get my own 100-mile split. I have improved my best time for 100 miles by about 35 minutes. In a burst of enthusiasm, I say to no one in particular: "Well, at least I've done a decent workout so far." There is laughter from some listeners although I hadn't meant to be humorous. Another bit of ice in me melts at having gotten this far. I yearn to catch up to Newton's 104-mile mark. He may have been broken finally, but I cannot move up a place till I get there. I think about the irreducibility of certain kinds of arithmetic. Oh, well, I decide, it'll come finally, just keep it going.

Jones and Bristol are ahead of me as the sky goes a deepish blue. A part of me yearns for a stronger sign of daylight. But even the knowledge that tomorrow is here seems remote—as does almost everything in the outside world. I do not know what I am thinking of: friends, numbers, ambitions—all that begins to fade. The replacement is a wider conviction that movement must and will go on.

Eight twenty-five in the morning brings me to 110 miles and third place. Jones is closing on Bristol, just twenty minutes ahead of him. I am now in new territory. Every step continues to make it the longest run of my life. Most of my companions look the worse for wear. Peter Hart is limping along, cheerfully giving me a verbal boost every time I go by. But he is walking dead on, no chance of his running again. It is a long time left to slog. Malcolm Campbell, who was finally persuaded at some ungodly hour to put on warmer clothes, has run bravely but at long last faded back to walking and slow running. Once when I am lapping him I ask how he's doing. "I'm running on memory," he says. Twenty minutes later he puts on a burst of speed that has him going faster than anyone else on the track. And so he goes, alternating between a crawl and a mean run.

During the dark hours, Knippenberg finally retired. Moilenan of Finland has been up and down all night, getting massage for his calves through his white knit longjohns and then pattering around again. Others walk and hardly anyone runs very fast anymore. One man gets to sit down on a chair and take a few drags on a cigarette while his taut-looking legs get massaged from several pairs of hands. Another man has his sweatpants pulled down while his wife works on his stringy white legs. His briefs are pulled askew and one pale buttock cheek gleams out upon the world, like a reject from a butcher's window. Thirteen have survived.

I have no appetite. I never did, after all. Cups of hot chicken noodle soup are nice. Cups of tea with milk and sugar and a

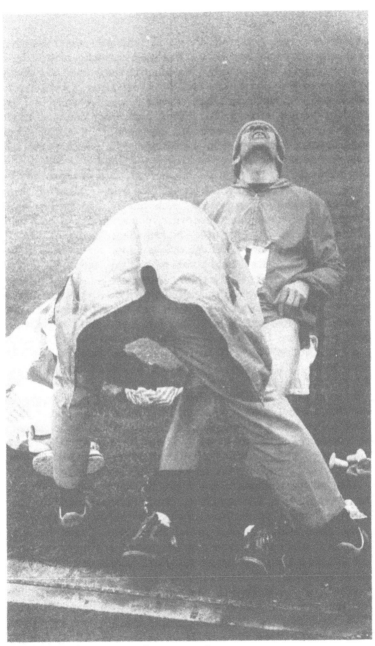

A handler tries to ease the cramps in a
runner's legs during a 24-hour race.

handful of grapes give a bit of a lift. Melanie asks about the meal of mashed potatoes and peas I had once carefully plotted in; I shake my head. I am getting a little cranky sometimes now about being asked if I want this or that. I miss my sister. I want her to return before I crack and start to walk. I spend a while figuring out how long it will take her to get back from London. About 10:45 she shows up and tells me how wonderful I look. That cheers me up. (Only a couple of days later do I learn how well she lied. As she saw us on the field she was reminded of Napoleon's rout from Moscow, but she was concerned not to let me know. "It never looked as though you were running freely," she said. "You were always holding yourself in check, but by morning you were just crawling around out there with your arms pulled high and jutting out to the side like little chicken wings." I had no idea. It was true at one point I had to go take a crap in the dressing room toilets. I debated whether to take a look at my face in the mirror on the way out—simply objective curiosity, as a medical student would study a burn victim so as to know for the next time. There was the matter of losing several seconds though. Nonetheless I looked and I had to laugh. I looked so bad—chalk white, new lines in the face, the quick aging you get when G-forces squash you out of shape. Ah, well. So I drank in hopefully the words of cheer from my little team. I forgot that they might be just saying it for my benefit.)

Even at London's Crystal Palace, Sunday morning involves a few things other than a 24-hour run into eternity. Through a fence beyond the scoreboard appear some young lads practicing field hockey. Like a child with its face to the bus window I stare with simple-minded wonder at the sight of new faces and actions. (When their practice is over they come to stare at us.)

After all the wildness of the night, the fog finally relents and the sun comes out. The sky clears, clouds blow away and the sun, bright and white, pours down on all of us although the air is still chilly. Bare arms and legs reveal themselves. There are four hours to go and now I am second. My recorder, John Legge (who had introduced himself before the race), comes down from the stands holding a little piece of paper. He waits for me at a quiet corner of the track. He has also run one of these monsters. He does not, however, appear to be capable of such madness. In his white cable sweater, casual slacks and glasses, below tumbled brown hair, he looks like a professor of economics on a Sunday afternoon in the park. His manner is quiet but his words are firm.

"You're simply pissing too much. You lose a minute every time

The author reaches 110 miles and finds the going getting harder.

you stop. Now this is quite interesting. You're in second place and Peddie is third, about eleven laps in back of you. All you have to do is keep running steadily, not faster, just steadily, and you have no idea how hard it is for someone to make up time on you. Just think about that."

I nod and run on. When I come around again he clocks me on his watch. On the third lap he breaks into the gentle trot needed to stay abreast and says: "You're doing just fine." It warms me to have an ally. Someone wants me to be second. It is like a strong voice coming from across the field that no one else can hear. This man has been through it; he knows, he has watched me all night, he radiates conviction as well as warning. I apply myself to my work, continue to bear down. Brusquely, like a reformed alcoholic anxious to prove his virtue, I now refuse drinks.

A tall, familiar figure smiles at me and hurries alongside as I creak past. It is close to eleven o'clock and Andy Milroy, fresh from pencil and paper and a stimulating night helping count laps, has news for me:

"In a little while you're going to set the American 200-kilometer record," he says.

I didn't even know there was such a thing.

"Are you sure?" I ask. "What about Park Barner—he's run further than where I'll get today, so he must have gone through faster."

Milroy shakes his head.

"No one took down his 200-k time so you're it. You'll break Corbitt's old mark of 20:59:41. Even if you walk you'll get it."

I ponder that for an instant. It seems odd to walk one's way to an American record—not quite what I had ever imagined in my heroic fantasies, but I wouldn't be choosy. I *would* walk to it if I had to. Luckily I'm still going, although (I hear later) what passed for a grin was actually a grimace. Sometimes I remember to unhook my face and bring my flapping arms down, but the feet are still moving. I get very happy about setting a record, though there are funny aspects to this record business you don't learn beforehand. To stand where no man stood before . . . Well, I'd found Coke signs in the Amazon jungle and ghostly footprints on the 200-k record, but I wasn't returning any gifts today.

They clock me in 20:14:04. I grow happier. I tell Joe and Melanie and my sister. I would have boasted to a wider circle but there are no other Americans around and I am not going to rub it in to Jack. He has got problems. Someone says that one of his

24

tendons is about to pop out of place. He is having bad trouble with his feet and he is walking slowly. It is not possible, perhaps, to walk any more slowly than Jack is walking but he stays cheerful. If I remember correctly, he offers a call or two of "Huffapuff!" It has been 16 hours or so since I heard *that*.

At 20:14:04 I go through the record for 200 kilometers, which is about 124.2 miles. I was never sure exactly which footstep did it, and the board took a while to get it up there. Well, I realize, I have to get back to just running.

The next goal becomes 130 miles. A note in the program states that only 24 athletes have run over 120 miles in 24 hours, and I know that each mile now will begin to place me higher in the world list rankings maintained by the English Road Runners Club. All the same, without even noticing exactly, I start to walk longish stretches. I am getting very tired of pushing. The steel bands my thighs are encased in have pinched my flesh so long that I am simply weary of being weary. I try little surges but I find myself breathing heavily just maintaining. My hair, which I had vowed not to cut until the race was over, is very long and curly. Although most of it is packed out of sight beneath a wool ski cap, long strands—limp with sweat and moisture from the nighttime fog—dangle in a Rastafarian manner on all sides. Some of the English handlers remind me that I should get a haircut when this thing is over. I won't forget, I say. Someone urges me to take off some of my sweat clothes but I am afraid of the cold—afraid of it the way you get when you're not able to stand the idea of shivering. Better to be damp and warm. My whole body feels so cramped and fed up that it can't take any more big surprises. Better now to live with myself the way I am. Even feeling better might be too big a surprise.

John Legge appears again. I brace myself for bad news.

"You're not doing badly," he says. "You can get to 140 miles or more if you just remember what I'm telling you about keeping some kind of speed up. You're really doing very well."

Okay, okay, I breathe to myself. One two three four. Push carry stumble bumble. On we go.

John waits again.

"Very good," he says.

Crashing and mumbling inside, I plow on as twigs and bones snap underfoot. Right foot is giving out now. Oh yes, a big fat seizure cramp is building. Pop out like Bristol. Tendon popping. The image is a little sickening. Well, never mind. Try picking up.

25

Oh Jesus, does that hurt. Forget it, we'll just back away a little now. Maybe I'll just ease off and walk. Well, I can't, there's John waiting for me. I'll show him I can run to where he is.

"Fine," he says.

That provides three seconds of warmth but then I face the back straight on my own.

Two miles to go to Ted Corbitt's record. Ted is a friend. (The first 24-hour I ever read about was when he went 134 miles, 782 yards in 1973 in England. I've heard him talk about it. It was the American record until Don Choi pushed it out a little further in 1978 and until Park Barner kicked it first to 152 plus, and finally to 162 plus, although all three runs are unofficial, according to RRC standards.)

Now that I am at 132½ miles, I am walking. I can't help it. Others tell me about Ted's record coming up. Some of the other runners know. Various people encourage me. "Great going," they say. I keep promising myself I will run to it but I keep putting it off. Perhaps I cannot. Then, with two laps to go, I feel that the only honorable way to pay homage to Ted's effort—and to appreciate it—is to feel it as deeply as I can, so I ram myself into a trot. It must look insane now. It has finally penetrated through to me that my version of running could be easily outwalked by a fast walker, but I guess I realize that there is nothing left to be ashamed of, nothing left to have false pride about. It is the best I can do.

It gets a little better actually as I go, although that may not mean much. Phew, one lap over. Good God, a whole other one now. I will break it into sections. Run this curve, just get through this. Fine, now down the straight. I keep laying mental track—not too much; don't overload the system—and I go through where I imagine the mark is and if there was time finally to rest and take it in I would cry. Maybe I do, in a half-strangled kind of way. So I have finally gotten somewhere. I don't know entirely why this is where it feels like I have done something but it is. I have no sense that I am better than Ted or that I have proven myself any stronger. Such an idea is talk from the other side of the line, thoughts that only an old self early in the venture would entertain. Out here the air is very thin. It doesn't matter exactly where I plant my flag in the snow. Anyone else who's climbed up to this vicinity knows what it means to wheeze for oxygen. We're pals.

"Good," John says, after he sees me hug a few people. "Now keep that up. Don't let your emotion make you lose sight of your work. You must keep moving. Walk if you must and then run. Come on."

I do try for a while, but I feel like I cannot do any more, very much more, than try not to crumble too quickly. Someone, probably Joe, has been appointed deputy after a conference among my friends, to tell me I was losing second and going down into third and soon after into fourth. This hardly surprises me. Peddie and I have been jabbering at each other a little bit about being so close. I hear a coach or a friend yelling at Gordon: "Pick it up, will you. The American's just four laps ahead of you."

I feel the equivalent of a grim smile. It's odd being "the American," being someone anyone would bother to chase. I find that I simply don't care. I want to get to Choi's mark now, and I grind along at a fairly brisk walk. If I could resist the attack of Peddie and Record I would, but since I can't perhaps I have no interest in my position anymore. One cares only about what one can do.

I reach Choi's mark around 23 hours. It is the last briar on the footpath I pluck away from my body. Barner's easygoing roll out 24 miles or so beyond where I am likely to get is impossibly far off. Now I am number-two American on the all-time list. I am exhausted—finally, truly and profoundly, and although I feel satisfaction it is dim compared to my present struggle.

"You must push on," John warns me. "Can't you run a little bit now?"

"I'll try," I say but I don't believe I can do it.

The loudspeaker announces that Gordon Peddie is now a half lap ahead of Shapiro. That stings me so I lurch into a duck-footed wobble. Straight pain on the thighs. There is no verbal equivalent for this and my mind, often so happy to chew on verbal models of the world, has nothing to say. Running now is like trying to swim far below the ocean surface. The pain is crushing. The world becomes a flow of gravity that pierces any attempt to sit up. No release, no relief, no easing of limbs will come now from attempting to run. Better now to give in and let the creeping current of a walk carry me a few yards further. It has occurred to me before the race that it would be reasonable to run 23 hours and just sit out the last hour. I consider it now. What more can I do? Is it worth pushing on in such a wretched state for the sake of a mile or so?

But the race *is* about distance covered and it *is* done however one looks doing it. John Legge is waiting again.

"Can't you run a little?" he asks.

Finally I am honest.

"I can't. My legs are absolutely shot."

"Okay," he says. "But keep going. You may have Peddie and Record ahead of you but they're not moving very fast. There's still a chance. This is where it matters, because later you'll wish you'd packed in a little more. You can still get to 140."

The scoreboard reads 1400 hours. One hour to go. Now that I have no hope of running, I can't imagine walking for another 60 minutes. No matter how agonizing an hour can be as a schoolboy, as the long-awaited bell never sounds, this is far worse. I think of just walking to 45 minutes to go and then I'll quit. It is the old game of sprinkling corn before a simple-minded self addicted to having hope. I pretend I have something to look forward to.

The support from the clumps of spectators is incredible.

"Come on, you're doing fabulous."

"Splendid running."

"Great."

A man clenching his fist and shaking it.

"Well done, lad."

It may be a mistake for a sufferer from frostbite to put his icy limbs next to a blazing heap of logs and then go out in the cold again. The spectators urge us on to more punishment. I am walking as fast as I can, aware at times that I must look maddened and ludicrous.

Peter Hart, stamping along like a weary version of Ahab on his little quarterdeck of Tartan track, has a foot that flaps madly out to one side. Campbell still puts on bursts. Record seems jolly and full of relative fire. At some point out there he gets the new Australian mark. Peddie claps me on the back and calls me matey—I quiver under such blows of friendship. Bristol makes his turtle way, looking as though he might go mildly on at his 2-mph speed into the next night. Moilenan is stamping firmly onward. Davie Jones, firmly in the lead, changes body color and begins to drift into fast walking as the hour wears by. He had a chance to get the world record for a while but he is on course for the 150's somewhere. We all talk a little to each other, but the work is still the same.

Forty-five minutes left. I feel dizzy and stumble sometimes. I put myself on the outer edge of the lane, anxious not to block anyone's progress by forcing them to go around. It means more distance for myself—even a handful of yards seem to weigh heavily at this point—but I don't care. A friend persuades me to relinquish my gloves. Less weight, they explain soberly. It seems a crazed attitude. My gloves have done very well by me so far.

John waits for me.

"Come on," he says.

I nod and say nothing. I need air. Who ever heard of wheezing at a walk, but that is what I am doing.

"You've had far less bad patch than anyone else out here," he says. "You've been very steady. Keep it going."

I might just about get cross now if I have to be pushed anymore. I snarl a little when offered drinks. Oh, God, this is so long. I never knew walking could be so tiresome. It is not pain I feel but sinking. My involvement with the world grows dimmer. It occurs to me that it would be nice to keel over. A barely audible whisper says it would be a way out. There is a longish period— from 40 minutes to go to 20 minutes to go—where it *is* truly a long time. Nothing is near at hand to sustain me. It seems not impossible but almost impossible to bother anymore, but I do. I do not know exactly how or why I do it but finally this spell is gone. When you go through a bad patch like that it feels like a dueling scar, a private one. Never afterward in your little war story can you be cheap about what a hero you were or how easy it was. Because it wasn't easy. It was a hard dimension, a stony place to travel through, neither more nor less. Nothing remarkable to enter, but it humbles one, burns off unnecessary fluff. (Later, remembrance will fade, leaving little trace of where you plunge underground like Alice into the rabbit hole.)

As fifteen minutes to go comes up I feel my entire body surge with the excitement. I ask again for my exact mileage. The motion is plodding and the breathing labored, but goddammit, I want every yard now. I can afford to pour out the last drops of reserve. The system shakes but holds steady. I grab the race program which contains a list of the top world-best performances and look to see who is within my grasp. Morelli of Italy, 220 kilometers. Unsuspectingly he dreams on his bed of ink and paper while I plod on to seize possession of his house. Pleasure for oneself can be cruelty toward another, but such philosophical regrets do not figure now.

Eight minutes to go. It sounds wonderful. It *is* wonderful. Soon it will be over. After such a long night, just stopping becomes a promise of great attraction.

Five minutes to go. Now we are all whipped up. The crowd calls out—"Come on! Now! You can do it! Let's go! Great job!" We respond as best we can. A maddened notion of trying to run

Weariness leaves its mark after hours of effort.

again seizes me. Well, why not. But let's not rush such things. I keep walking as fast as I possibly can. Anything can be tolerated now. (Although I do not notice it, I learn later that some of those who watch are crying. And some of the recorders who labored so long to keep track of their flock cry as well.)

Three minutes. There is something lovely happening now, the general awareness of the brevity of all time—long or short, the funny, madcap, unbelievable adventure coming at last to a close. (Adam, a friend, has said the day before that he wondered about the worth of such a venture. Later, after witnessing the will that drove the scrambling, strung-out mob forward in the last few moments, he says that it may not have much meaning beyond what it was in terms of ordinary worth, but that it was worth doing for its own sake. I have been inside as a runner and outside as a spectator, watching long runs come to an end. I know it is very special.)

I lumber past Jack. We give each other a quick sideways hug and then I am off to get a few more meters in.

Two minutes to go. I break into a maddened canter, the weakened superstructure teetering, the cordage of tendons and muscles creaking like rigging under a too-full sail. But the barge holds, noses forward. God, how people are yelling.

One minute to go. This is happiness, if I stop to think about it, but now I just feel it. Mad as a hatter, I go around the curve past the yelling faces. Someone runs toward me with an orange traffic cone, the final marker of my voyage. A gun fires and the cone goes down—kerplunk! I stop a stride or two later and bend forward, hands on knees, chest heaving. I utter some strangled, half-broken sobs and then, at last, the long-sought release comes. The tide of emotion lifts the forlorn boat out of the mudbanks. I paddle around in my little puddle of joy. Isn't it nice to feel so good! Down the backs of my legs comes a strong physical feeling of release and warmth. There are hugs, pictures, handshakes, congratulations all around. Word comes that I have covered 138 miles, 1,228 yards, for fourth place. It is not 140 miles and it is not a lot of other things, but for what it is I am profoundly grateful and content. I am content at last.

There is no rapid anticlimax. The survivors clump in toward a bench. Jones, a blue-lipped winner at 153 miles, 1,143 yards, holds his Percy Cerutty trophy aloft and drinks some ale from it. We pass it around, medieval warriors sampling mead. Jones gives a little speech. A bank of faces closes in on every side. It is a happy close among friends.

Adam drives me back to the hotel, and after a hot tub and some food I am left alone to sleep. Only—as I knew from before—there will be no sleep. Toenails are bloated loose from their moorings. Broken clumps of blisters between the toes and the harsh drone of overtaxed feet and shins make sleepiness a torment. Ending the race is just the beginning. The body claims its due and, for now, only rest and healing matter. The cave is beckoning, and when I get home snow will soon be falling perhaps. After the hunt, I shall be licking my wounds, waiting until driven by hunger to go out again on the long chase.

Final Results

1.	D. Jones	Blackburn Harriers	153m	1143y
2.	J. Record	AUSTRALIA	142	1614
3.	G. Peddie	Epsom and Ewell Harriers	140	1219
4.	J. Shapiro	USA	138	1228
5.	F. Thomas	Chelmsford A.C.	135	1133
6.	D. Attwell	Altrincham A.C.	133	448
7.	M. Campbell	Notts. A.C.	128	1333
8.	M. Moilenan	FINLAND	127	1605
9.	C. Bristol	USA	125	1031
10.	K. Shaw	Cambridge Harriers	123	633
11.	B. Slade	Exeter Harriers	122	1497
12.	R. Holmes	Notts. A.C.	112	1617
13.	P. Hart	Leamington Cycling & A.C.	108	684
14.	M. Newton	South London Harriers	104	1561
15.	J. Knippenberg	NETHERLANDS	89	840
16.	D. Ritchie	Forres Harriers	54	1197
17.	B. Harney	Rotherham Harriers	43	1310

The author celebrates 138 miles 1228 yards
with his sister and his handler.

Cahit Yeter congratulates Rich Langsam
after a 50-mile race, New York, 1978.

2.
LEARNING TO RUN THE LONG HAUL

1.
What Is an Ultramarathon?

How long is a marathon?

Worldwide the standard marathon distance is 26 miles and 385 yards, a distance based on whimsical historical circumstance:

The world's first so-called "marathon" race took place in the 1896 Olympics in Athens, the first modern-day Olympiad ever held. Historical legend credits the herald Pheidippides with a run from the Greek battlefield of Marathon to the city of Athens. Pheidippides purportedly gasped out his message of the Athenian victory over the invading Persians and then fell dead. In 1894 a French scholar tugged at the elbow of Baron Pierre de Coubertin, the founder of the modern Olympics, and suggested a race in commemoration of Philippides. That marathon and the early ones that followed, both in the Olympics and elsewhere, varied a bit in length, although they were usually about 24–25 miles long.

At the 1908 Olympics in London, the marathon race began at Windsor Castle and ended in front of the Royal Box in White City Stadium, a distance which happened to be 26 miles and 385 yards. In 1936 that was officially settled upon as the precise distance required for a foot race to be called a marathon.

How long is an ultramarathon?

Technically an ultramarathon is any foot race longer than a marathon. All the same, races that cover only 50 or 60 kilometers (a marathon is 42.195 kilometers) really have more of the character of a marathon than an ultra. Normally the word "ultramarathon" refers to races which are, at the minimum, about twice as long as a marathon; 50 miles, 100 kilometers (62.137 miles) or 100 miles are the most common distances both in America and abroad. An ultramarathon is a race beyond the normal ken, not only in terms of mileage but of time spent on a road or track in ceaseless forward motion—five hours, six hours, eight hours or longer. And the journey runners who run vast distances across continents spend not just one day covering 50 miles but a string of consecutive days—an altogether different kind of struggle than the road racer who can run flat-out and then rest on the morrow.

There are also runs against the clock in the ultraworld where the object is to cover the greatest amount of distance possible in a given time span. The most popular of these rare events in modern times are the 24-hour races where competitors manage, with but brief pauses for toilet and eating, to run and walk the entire time.

Ultrarunners can be a precise, indeed a fanatically precise lot. Although there are point-to-point races of varying lengths—72 miles around Lake Tahoe, for example, or 54 miles, 460 yards from London to Brighton—ultra races usually comprise distances that terminate in zeroes, testimony to the inclination of the human mind to be fascinated by the perfect order of those rounded-off, almost mystical units of measurement. Surely a course of 99 kilometers is as fierce a test as running 100, but I never expect to see such a race take place.

When the tiny clan of these unpaid, unencouraged, unsung amateur runners gets word of some new feat that's been pulled off—somebody doing 160-odd miles in 24 hours, say, or running through Death Valley and back again nonstop, they might well feel a stir of excitement and a dash of envy, wondering if they, too, could do such a thing. But every one of them knows the cost of such feats, remembering from personal experience the inexorable price in commitment and concentration. It is high. An ultrarunner cannot just drift through a 100-miler, thinking of something else for 10 long hours. Somehow the normal little cycles of rest and play, working and eating, must be consumed by the steady fire within, a fire that burns strongly only if tended to without lapse by mind and body.

Even when I have been away from long-distance running for a while, I can still remember just how hard it can be. The stress of such efforts burns off all but the deepest reasons for going on. There is left only the driving edge of oneself called will or hunger and everyone understands it a little differently for themselves. And these efforts, too, depend on frail bones and tired feet. The romance of the calling is never far away from worries about a blood blister or an unhappily full colon.

Ultrarunning is a sport which remains for the most part undiscovered by the mob. On race day ultrarunners straggle in, nodding and chatting to one another and complaining like sly horse traders about the poor condition of their joints. Mostly they know each other well. Like anything else that people share together, there comes out of the experience a sense of support, camaraderie and humor about hammering away for so long at such an enterprise.

And there is always the vision of new frontiers for these restless pioneers. The times keep improving, the distance in the 24-hour races stretch outward every few years, and there are always different cities to run between that no one else has ever tried. There is, always, the chance to do not only what very few can do but what is new for yourself—say, run 50 miles and manage to finish. These extra-long-distance runners actually like to feel good so they are willing for the sake of a little spiritual satisfaction to put up with being tired and sometimes in pain. I think, also, that the potential of our neighbors communicates itself. When I hear, for example, that Don Choi has been staging 48-hour races on a track in California, it remains in my mind as a reminder of the extra stretch I myself might make if I cared to.

Inevitably, of course, the faces you see at these races tend to change. Ultramarathoning is not to everyone's taste and sometimes a race or two is enough to satisfy curiosity. Injuries, too many years without stretching, other interests, the difficulty of really staying fit year after year at a high level of enthusiasm—all these things lead many ultrarunners away from the contest, but there are always the outstanding exceptions.

I so not mean to suggest ever that a subtle superiority wraps itself like some heroic mantle around the shoulders of the ultra buffs who go on. Comparisons claiming that one sport is the most difficult or most remarkable or most truly illustrative of human endurance strike me as offensive. Such comparisons are not meaningful; effort and enthusiasm will always impress the spectator and sustain the competitor. The extravagance of ultrarunning needs no extra adornment. And like any collection of varied personalities some ultrarunners are to one's taste and others not. Malicious gossip and sour thoughts about one's rivals are not so uncommon, for ultrarunning is in most respects a thoroughly competitive sport where the strength and speed you exhibit is yours alone. No teammates are about with whom to dilute the blame or praise. And yet as a group I do feel that ultrarunners are for the most part an extremely congenial and relaxed bunch. The worn cliché about introverted long-distance runners always strikes me as comical when I witness their magpie chatter in bars or pubs or on a run, or even while shivering beneath blankets, retailing through chattering teeth the dramatic events of a just-finished epic run . . .

2.
Why We Run the Ultras

Why do we do it?

The idea always comes first. It begins, as it must, as a perverse whim that offends the ordinary commonsense. But it is a bit of inspiration, a diamond grain in the shoe that demands an itch.

Put men on the boards and run 'em around for six days without stopping; send 'em in from the coast of the Indian Ocean up over those young mountains to faraway Maritzburg; line 'em up in Los Angeles and nurse them over the bitterly bad roads of two generations ago. Such feats were once rare. Some races died out after one or two tries, but sometimes they took hold and flourished and became enshrined as yearly classics that ultra enthusiasts could set themselves up against as a kind of measure of their own strength and determination.

But they all depended for a start on the likes of some very unlikely men who, for one reason or another, loved to be nursemaids and promoters of ultra events. There was Sir John Astley for one, a nineteenth-century member of Parliament, with his penchant for a droll phrase and money in the pocket. And there was Ernest Neville, whose portly but dynamic frame draped in a black greatcoat was a fixture at ultraraces; because of his inspired badgering a group of men stood shivering beneath Big Ben, thirty years ago on a soaking wet dawn, before plunging down the slippery roads to the distant sea.

It comforts me to know that there have always been agents around to carry out the will-o'-the-wisps of these dreamers—your garden variety back-door runners of both immense and little talent who were willing to try. Let there be word of such an event and most people will merely smile in disbelief. But some will always come forward to see what they can do—even if it's just enough to be called racing. In the last five years, running great distances has become increasingly popular. Away from the spotlight of the world's interest, this accumulation of splendid cranks flourishes in its own carry-on-regardless style. Ultraraces teach much to all who watch and run them, and cost far less than dives beneath the

42

sea or expeditions up the face of Annapurna. Why, I myself was a kind of unwitting godfather to a great race in my hometown of New York City, the first to give a startled blessing to an idea that might have come to nothing. It is a story that begins two years ago.

I could hear the urgency in his voice when he said he had to talk to me. It was winter and by the time we met in midtown Manhattan as prearranged, the sky was long since dark and the wind bitterly cold. We were running in opposite directions along Second Avenue, tucking in a few more miles whenever the chance presented itself. Everyone has a distinctly unique running style so it was easy enough to recognize Richie Innamorato pumping his way up the avenue from blocks away when all I could spy was a head, a bouncing dot above the speeding traffic. He must have been a sight the year before, I thought, when he ran down the East Coast from Maine to Florida.

There were no preliminaries and barely had I reversed direction when I asked what was wrong.

There was nothing wrong, he said, but he had a new idea. His voice rose without effort, booming off the buildings of Second Avenue. Passersby eavesdropped willy-nilly on our conversation, turning to stare at our two figures running past in long underwear and watch caps at ten o'clock at night. Richie's moods can change rapidly, but I had never seen him so excited.

"I want to put on a hundred-miler," he yelled, his arms waving. "It'll be fabulous! The New York Hundred. Oh, it could be a classic, Jimmie."

He rattled off possible locations—Governor's Island, Staten Island, Central Park, a track on the East River Drive—and provided an accompanying dissertation on their possible advantages and flaws in terms of accessibility, nighttime lighting, freedom from crowds and muggers, and so on. He had clearly been studying the maps. The fever of his brainchild was upon him and at one point he whooped with excitement. He was so beside himself I could hardly encourage him to any greater pitch of enthusiasm, but it did seem an exciting—if scary—idea.

For of course we would both run the race ourselves. We knew very few people indeed who had ever run 100 miles. It had both the lure and the gloom of unknown territory. We toted up the names of a dozen surefire crazies likely to relish such an attempt, and thus the race was born. Innamorato's theretofore hidden talent as an ultra organizer and promoter finally had a chance to surface.

43

After completing **44** loops around a pond in a New York City park, Don Ritchie has a new world's record for 100 miles on the road.

He had run a number of them himself, and he remembered everybody he'd ever met at an ultra race, as well as a startling number of their best times at various distances. And for something he cared about he was relentless and a perfectionist.

He even managed to control his habit of always being an hour late and the following summer, to my disbelief, he was there early to see the first annual New York Unisphere Invitational 100-miler go off exactly on time. The 7 runners who went on to the end to finish, out of the 22 who started, comprised what was then the largest field of 100-mile finishers ever in the U.S. The bevy of new times forced Nick Marshall of Camp Hill, Pa., himself one of the finishers, to revise his list of the top twenty 100-mile times in America. It was one of a number of all-time lists that Marshall, the unofficial doyen of ultra statistics in the U.S., maintains and distributes every year. There was a lot of satisfaction and excitement about the race in the East Coast ultraworld and eventually the wires were abuzz again with plans for the second annual version.

That went off on the evening of June 15, 1979, and ended the following day. After almost 12 hours of nonstop running which ended when he snapped the tape, a shy, red-bearded schoolteacher from Scotland found he could no longer even walk. Donald Andrew Ritchie, 34, better known to his grammar-school students by such names as Beedy, Carrot and Noah, was carried to a chair so he could dunk his long white feet in ice water, one of the most immediate and gratifying rewards for having set a new world's record hardly anyone in the world even knew existed—11 hours, 51 minutes and 11.6 seconds to cover 100 miles on the road. A small, awestruck crowd gathered around just to stare, and the man whose mother has to pry out of him the news that he's won a race suddenly found himself a minor celebrity.

Ritchie, who also holds the world's best performance on the track for 100 miles (11:30:51), had lost all sensation in his blistered and tormented feet hours before. Although there was a portable toilet set up near the checkpoint of the 2.3-mile loop course (44 circuits were required to complete the distance), Ritchie had simply urinated as he ran in the darker, unfrequented sections of the course. It was a trick he picked up from Frank Bozanich, a California ultrarunner with whom he was sharing a room at the Mayflower Hotel. Frank had chased the Scotsman in the early stages of the race until the near 6-minute-per-mile pace broke the challenge and Bozanich retired from the competition.

Ritchie ran on alone through the night, his pace deteriorating slowly after 30 miles until he rallied somewhat between 85 and

100 miles. Unlike the cool coastal weather of his native northern Scotland, the temperature lingered at an oppressively hot and humid level. I served as Ritchie's handler, waiting for him on each lap, knowing by the large digital clock almost to the second when to expect him to appear around the bend of the path.

He had prepared two drinks in advance. One was ERG, a commercial preparation which replaces electrolytes and salts lost from the body. The other was a special mix of long-chain glucose polymers which would be rapidly absorbed from the gut into the bloodstream. He provided me with a small, narrow-necked bottle with instructions to alternate each kind of drink on successive laps. I fell into stride as he ran through and handed off the bottle from his right side—Ritchie is right-handed—so he wouldn't have to reach across his chest and break his gait.

Earlier in the day he had muttered something uncharacteristically sour about the mental deficiency of someone who persisted in handing him a sponge from the left several laps in a row. (The most easygoing ultrarunner in private life may frequently turn testy under the hammer of pushing toward the goal.) Ritchie wasn't inclined to say much when he was working hard. He chugged from the bottle and returned it with monotonous regularity at a point about 400 yards down the pathway. A wet sponge to dab his high, balding brow, a swab on his thighs, a slap at the thick clouds of gnats which drifted like black mist out of the tall grass surrounding the pond, and with a word of encouragement from me he was off, sawing wood again, arms pumping, shoulders hunching more and more deeply as with each succeeding lap the familiar weariness set in.

At one point when someone asked how he felt, he said: "It's just survival." He never smiled, never acknowledged the yells or the pattering applause when he churned beneath the blazing night lamps which had been set up for the officials and timekeepers. Those stalwart volunteers fueled themselves on jelly donuts, coffee and the hypnotic lure of the race. There was nothing miraculous to learn here from contact with a great athlete, nothing startling except that it was a matter of concentration—that narrow, arduous bridge between wanting and getting.

There were others there, too, from whom one could learn. For, as if Ritchie's startling excesses were not enough, twenty-six other runners had gathered together late in the afternoon the previous day to see if they, too, could scramble up such slippery slopes. The ultragang, mostly members of the East Coast division, had taken time off from nursing bruised and injured bodies and

Scotland's Don Ritchie keeps up a hard early pace, even in a 100-miler.

driven in from the different boroughs of New York and from neighboring states. A few local runners came in early from work for the seven p.m. start and rode out on the subway, clutching their athletic carry-bags much the way astronauts haul oxygen packs on their way to the launch tower. Only as the subway doors opened at the Shea Stadium stop, they gave no waves of farewell on their way to this space trip. (No one would have understood them.)

There had been other petitioners seeking admission to the sacred grove. Imploring letters had been delivered to the Queens home of Innamorato, but Richie was not allowing any old chicken from the barnyard to rush forward to offer its neck to the 100-mile blade. Only those who gave real proof of "seriousness" were allowed to run. "This is not a carnival," he said. Qualifying times were established to weed out any who might hurt themselves by trying something they weren't ready for, or who hadn't the potential to finish within the time limit. One letter of rejection never reached a runner in Germany. The man flew in anyway and once arrived, what could be done? Anyone that serious deserved a chance, and as it turned out the runner acquitted himself honorably.

So did others. Almost eight hours after Donald Ritchie finished his record-breaking run, the last of the 11 who eventually went the whole distance came across the line under the pitiless summer sun. And among the 16 others who quietly chucked it at various points along the way—one man quit after running 88 miles—there was much to witness and admire. None of the competitors felt very good about a d.n.f.—a did-not-finish—when the whole point was to go the entire 100, but among the few of us who gathered together to keep watch through the night, it was clear enough that even running 30 or 40 or 75 miles was something worthwhile. And perhaps (as one more of the generally unspoken but shared understandings among ultrarunners and fans— numbering among the smallest of any sport in the world) there was wafted abroad that special air of attentiveness and respect when such a violent assault on ordinary boundaries is attempted.

I remember seeing the massive back of my friend, Brian Jones. As he strode toward the spot where his gear had been stowed, he was wearing only blue shorts and a ridiculous little terrycloth cap pulled tightly down on his head which he soaked with water. A few friends and handlers clustered about him—did he want that? need this? Through the evening, the survivors who touched down out of their night flight for refueling had various odd requests: an aspirin, a change of socks, a calf massage; and wanting, sometimes, some words of advice or cheer. There was a little humor and something affecting in seeing such intense knots of civilians clustering about the soldiers with their single-minded, almost child-like absorption in their effort.

I felt a twinge of envy at having chosen not to run the race again that year—in the middle of such an effort you draw a little bit from the attentiveness of others. You, too, figure in an effort that everyone has agreed—although none can quite explain why—is important. True enough that it's ephemeral and that no one may later remember that you finished in 14 or 15 or 16 hours, in the back of the pack.

Two days later I helped Ritchie carry a 4½-foot-high trophy, presented to him by Sri Chinmoy and some of his followers. The United Nations meditation master had been present at the race much of the night, dressed in a red jogging suit, seated silently in a canvas chair, his chin on one hand, his knees wiggling as he watched the ghostly figures run past. At a testimonial dinner on the night after the race, Chinmoy's group sang songs in Ritchie's honor, much to his embarrassment. I awkwardly raised aloft the golden streamer-festooned trophy as Ritchie and I walked along Central Park West, like the leaders of some Hindu votive procession. Passersby and doormen stared in mild wonderment, but Ritchie was no visiting soccer star or baseball hero and remained unrecognized.

The rewards from the world are small, in spite of such an occasional gaudy exception, so why do these men and the occasional women who run in the ultras put themselves through such long hours of difficulty? It's a familiar question once you're in trouble in the middle of a race, when going on defies the deep common sense of the body—which always craves comfort. The part of oneself that dares ask 'why' is engaging the other parts in more than a theoretical discussion. The answer that emerges will decide whether you walk off onto the grass and end the pain, or somehow accommodate your aching body to its heavy intrusion instead.

Surprisingly, the press was there with cameras and notepads— including *The New York Times*, heady homage indeed. Only in South Africa—which gives in to an annual fever of enthusiasm over the 54-mile Comrades Marathon—does any nation's press pay much attention to such goings-on. And this is nothing new. With the exception of the 6-day races in the late nineteenth century, newspaper files yield absolutely nothing on ultras. Even the electronic console at the Library of Congress in Washington, D.C., which cast its green-and-black printout before my gaze during my research, could not mine a single book on ultrarunning from its depths. Nor in the recent riot of running books unleashed upon the public can one find any mention of ultras except in passing.

I could find only a small cluster of exceptions to this dearth. Arthur F. H. Newton, the father of ultrarunning in this century, printed four slender books* during his years of retirement in England. The last two were paid for out of his own pocket, and they were not easily traced. A library in California had one book and the New York Public Library another. According to its card catalog, the British Museum supposedly had the other two but they were then missing somewhere among its infinitude of volumes. Booksellers who claimed to specialize in search missions smiled contemptuously at my interest in sports. It took two years, two trips to England and the aid of a Xerox machine before I could track down all four volumes which together provide an amusing, fascinating and still relevant mixture of advice on ultra training, as well as an inside look at the long-ago classics of the 1920's and 30's when tennis sneakers and lionhearted indifference to rutted and stony roads characterized an even tinier band of crazies than exists nowadays.

And now ultras looked to soon be enfolded in the same hot media embrace reserved for marathons—which are still treated less as sport than as a giant be-in of human interest stories. The simple drama of a race is replaced by foolish gutterings on "runner's high." How long, I wondered, could the simple folk I saw around me withstand the lure of batting lashes and fatuous questions? That subtle flavor of elitism, of peace and elbow room with neighbors you knew, who could say how much longer that would last? The irony of my own involvement in rolling aside the rock from the cave entrance by writing this very book did not escape me. It just depended on your point of view about such things.

Five years earlier, as a member of the venerable B.A.A. (Boston Athletic Association) running club, I visited the club's guiding light, crusty Jock Semple, in his tiny physiotherapy office in a corner of the perpetually seedy Boston Garden. Jock bore down

---

Common Sense Athletics, The Publisher, 1932; *Running*, Witherby, 1935; *Running in Three Continents*, Witherby, 1940; *Races and Training*, Bainbridge, 1949.

on knots in my calves as we discussed one of his then favorite young running stars, Max White, who as a tenderfoot 23-year-old had run a fine fourth in the London-to-Brighton race. Jock shook his balding head in dismay, his Scots burr undimmed by some forty years in the States.

"Why, for the love of Pete, does he want to run such things? That ultra stuff is for old men, fellas at the end of their running careers. There's no future in it, none a t'all. Why it's a disgrace how the Boston papers don't even print a paragraph on it—and a local boy, too. Nobody cares about such stuff. He should run marathons—that's where the glory is. Why run these things if you don't get proper credit?"

Jock had fingered both the appeal and the limitation of ultrarunning in a way—there is room in it for the slower folk to shine out a little more clearly. Conversely, the most talented speed merchants of the marathon would not want to sell their wares in a non-Olympic sport like ultrarunning. (The marathon is the longest foot race held at the Olympic Games.) Shop talk among ultrarunners in this respect is the same the world over: what would happen when the 2:10 or 2:12 marathon runners put their minds to the 50-mile record?

The most successful ones have no need, no incentive to push further out to the ultra distances. Ultra territory is shadowy. Information about it is sparse. Bill Rodgers has said he's intrigued by it but will wait till later in his career. Frank Shorter has the notion that it's bigger, heavier musclemen who take on such things. Besides, he said, he loves running every day too much to stand a week or two of hobbling around after a protracted effort of that kind. But perhaps speed in the shorter races like the marathon doesn't mean the same runner would do well in the longer monsters such as the 100-milers.

"You don't know until they try, do you?" points out Cavin Woodward, an Englishman who owns a pair of the fastest feet in the ultra business. "It's possible that when these fast blokes get into a race and run at a 5-minute-per-mile pace, they don't have time to think about anything else. Whereas when you try to run in ultras, then you've got plenty of time and you've got to have something to think about. Maybe they wouldn't be able to. Jim Dingwell and Don McGregor were two of Scotland's best at one time in marathons, but put them in a 36-miler and they're completely different. Stick them on the track for 62-odd miles and they'll be even worse."

But as Cavin's wife Carol points out, her husband's habit of saying after an ultra, "Well, I wouldn't've won it if so-and-so had been there, because he's faster," isn't the point. Running is satisfyingly final and clean-cut that way. On the given day only those who show up to try themselves against each other can be judged. Only one can win. The rest is speculation.

But for then, when the New York ultra was at its zenith, the present was good enough. It was nice just to be there among the forty or so folk, many of whom knew each other from before and whose easy manners made the steps of the abandoned 1939 World's Fair amphitheater, especially after nightfall, resemble the campfire grounds of a tribe of gypsies. Tucked off in the shadows away from the string of lights, a few exhausted runners and officials lay curled up like children with their hands slipped between their knees. Cardboard cards with each runner's number dangled from a long clothesline suspended between the immense concrete pillars. Beneath were stashed rucksacks, shopping bags and ice coolers that held extra changes of clothes and running shoes. Bottles of soda and other more elaborate concoctions were dunked in ice. The stinging incense of Ben Gay hung in the air.

Here and there small groups sat on the steps chatting about the race. An occasional stranger would wander in out of the night, drawn like a moth by the brightly lit scene, wondering aloud: "A hundred miles! You're kidding. Gee." And stay an hour or so. Where did these wanderers come from at such godforsaken stretches of the night, when even dawn seemed too remote to be real?

But then this was New York. Up by the official's table were watchers who called out the numbers of the approaching runners so that the checkers could bend forward over the immense swathes of cardboard art paper, whose carefully ruled-off squares plotted the progress of so many ships bound for port. Joe Kleinerman, the brassy-voiced veteran of many such races, who's been involved in running one way or another for fifty years, piloted the whole affair with his sometimes brusque but always precise style.

It was strange not to be running myself but I had a chance to learn what it was like to watch from the outside—which is just as tiring in its way! I remembered how much it meant to come around out of the ghostly spell of two miles of running past empty park benches, out among the trees with the branches that made you duck, the bright moon, the smell of the water, and finally, after coming up over a small rise on a bridge, seeing the first slice of lamplight from the timers' table gleaming ahead like a welcoming beacon. I always ran a little smoother and faster then. Tonight I could see how so many of the runners began to weary and age, shrugging when asked how they were doing, cracking grim jokes or ignoring the question altogether if it was getting too bad.

Perpetually good-natured Dean Perry, who organizes the ultraclassic around Lake Waramaug in Connecticut every year, was sporting a black beard. He ran flatfooted early on, far more laboriously than normal. He hoped to just gut it out but eventually had to quit. Bill Lawder, known among pals as the New Jersey lunatic because of his insatiable appetite for running ultras, was another dropout.

There was slightly built Jack Bristol, 29, another Connecticut native, mustachioed, always wearing a wry smile and, like a professional mercenary, always showing up where the action is—in the past year I had met him at the foot of the stairwell of the Empire State Building, the foot of Big Ben in London and on the Verrazano Bridge just before the start of the New York City Marathon. He went on to finish sixth in 16:24:03.

There were others I didn't know but who became familiar, such as Lion Caldwell, 28, from Dallas, Texas, who was greeted by his blonde wife every time his lanky body with its tanned, sharply etched musculature appeared. His skin was drawn tight as drumskin but he went on to finish second in 13:33:46.

And of course the man who never misses a 50-miler or a 100-kilo or any other megadistance, and regularly does some intercity jaunts of his own, was there. The legendary Park Barner—fresh from a massive effort two weeks earlier on a California track where he set a new, unofficial world's record of 162 miles, 537 yards—steamed past, the long action of his arms and legs never seeming to tire much. Park's usual taciturnity was mellower than usual and he chatted a bit with handlers or other runners he passed. People commented on it. "Park's talkative tonight," they said, as farmers might mention a small change in the weather. Perhaps there'd been too many runs in the past year—too many 50-milers, one 200-mile nonstop intercity run, a 24-hour track run in New Jersey, whatever—but one of Park's legs hemorrhaged a bit. (After the race, uncharacteristically, he took a week off from running.)

Slowly the runners finished—and continued to drop off—one by one. As the sun rose it was clearly becoming another sweltering summer day. At long last John Kenul trotted over the line 19 hours and 44 minutes after it all began. The pennants, the digital clock and the plastic buckets that had been used for water were stored away in car trunks. The pathway around the pond was no longer a magic circle, and ordinary strollers promenaded over the

55

asphalt, unaware of the ever-so-serious rule that had governed the ordinary ground a little while before: that all grown children running in circles could not stray from the path. The once orange moon of the night still hung overhead, pale and sobered, not hinting at how wild a night it had witnessed. All around the city, the few dozen racers went to sleep, scattered again until the call of the next enterprise.

3.
With a Measure of Stubborn Perversity

Ultramarathoners are really ordinary folk in their private lives, these men and occasional women who run from coast to coast across the U.S.; stampede up torturous hills in an annual South African 54-miler; or pick their way alone with a flashlight along 186.4 miles of towpath and road in the C & O Canal race. Ultrarunners are simply afflicted with heavy doses of stubborn perversity, driven forward by a gnawing complex of motivations that sometimes are most easily and most truly explained in the simple statement that we run so far simply because we love to do it—or need to do it.

After the deluge of books and articles that repeat ad nauseam the virtues of health and spiritual enlightenment to be found in trotting along with one's own two feet, it is perilous now to advance claims of superiority for ultrarunners as a class of people. Ultrarunners are usually (not always) a relatively modest and certainly neglected group of athletes whose motivation is about as "clean" as one can witness in sport. Of course, there are a few silver geegaws and cups, and the appearance of the runners' names on lists that only we—and a few tolerant friends—ever bother to read. We remain an almost invisible tribe, tiny in numbers, ghostly "superachievers" who are recognizable on sight only to each other. Nothing in demeanor or musculature suggests the sustained and gorgeous lunacy of which we are capable.

Why, even a great one like New York City's Ted Corbitt, former marathon Olympian and American record holder until recently for 24 hours (134 miles, 782 yards), possesses a running style that makes strangers blanch. The contorted face and ungainly idiosyncrasies that accompany his gait cause more than a few unwitting observers to write him off as a threat. Corbitt's modesty and social shyness run deep; he talks swiftly and quietly, really mumbling at times. But it only takes a question or two—say, about the 24-hour effort—and the vivid scars surface. "It was like a nightmare," he recalled of his 18-hour bout with cramp and fatigue. And suddenly the stern will and the strict judgment he passes over his "less successful" runs flash out.

Among the unsung legion of runners in the rear who provide the background for the achievement of the winners can be found John Kenul, a postal clerk from Brooklyn. Kenul's running style is a modest trot. His leg muscles betray no extraordinary development or hint of his modest but endlessly bulldog endurance. His running garb is not of the nylon-and-flash school, and I have rarely seen him without a funny old cap on his head.

I first met John on an overheated local train from Philadelphia to Harrisburg in 1977 on the way to a 100-kilometer race. His gear was stowed in a large plastic leaf bag and he was just different enough from everyone else in the car to make me guess—accurately, as it turned out—that he, too, was headed for the race. He finished that race—as he finishes all the races he starts—long after almost everyone else was in, never losing his quiet good humor. In 1979 he ran two 100-milers within the space of a week—one in Virginia over a back-country trail, and the other in New York.

In this sport appearances don't matter too much. Not just because they can be deceptive but because even the less gainly, the less fluid, the dreamers like the poet with the long flowing beard who runs in jeans in order "to make a statement," or even the clowns who just hoot along at the rear, can all be accommodated. The distances are so long that simply to cover them can be for some an achievement that matters much more than the speed with which it is done.

I find it ironic that some of my ultra acquaintances ridicule my habit of measuring my runs around Manhattan. I do it with an expensive Swiss-wheeled map reader along topographical maps pinned to the wall of my apartment, so I can know how far I've run within a hundredth of a mile. To get their finishing time in a race, they calculate with blinding dexterity minute-per-mile pace formulas. Like enchanted dervishes, their lips flutter as they half mumble their way through a briar patch of multiplication and long division in order to pronounce a few seconds later: "At this pace, we only have another five hours to go!" Cheering news for comrades slogging fifty miles up the Hudson River valley on a training run!

Scarcely less demonic than these birds of flight—from a mathematical viewpoint—are the ground fowl who scramble relentlessly below, tracking the longest of flights with unerring, almost ruthless

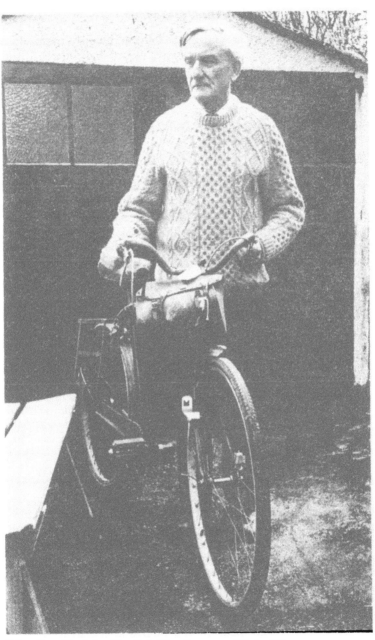

John Jewell of the English Roadrunners Club still
uses the late Arthur Newton's bicycle for measuring courses.

precision. For as much as it fascinates some to run these tremendous distances, it fascinates others to watch, record and collate. It is in this realm of standardization, precise course measurement and careful checking for lapses that the English have shone forth in the post–World War II era, a veritable lighthouse of integrity. Officials of the English Road Runner's Club sit in stern judgment before admitting ultrarace times onto their world list.

John Jewell, corresponding secretary for the English RRC, is one of these inspired worriers. On a recent visit to England, I traveled out to his home in Wokingham, a small town forty miles outside of London perched among the easy roll of a countryside that still boasts a fair amount of trees and grassland. Jewell quickly fished out several letters from correspondents around the world and asked what I knew about this solo effort, or that race, so that he might resolve some doubts about the accuracy of miles covered. And this was only one of a number of times he sought to test, like the chemist he once was, the purity of a purported performance.

In the cozily crowded living room of his home is an enclosed glass bookcase that gives evidence of his travels to Iran and India, where he once lived. There are back issues of a Himalayan journal, an old volume of *Half Hours in Field and Forest* and copies of books by Arthur "Greatheart" Newton, the shy, self-effacing, rabbity-looking gent with spectacles and pipe who so revolutionized ultrarunning. (Newton's shadow still falls far in England among the older generation who once knew him.) Out in back Jewell keeps a black Hercules bicycle Newton used to ride during cycling trips and still uses to measure courses, a touching example of appropriateness and British thrift.

Jewell fished among the well-organized wealth of papers in his study drawers (which I yearned to plunge into myself) and handed me a mimeoed form. It was the RRC's application for recognition of a race as being "World Best Performance." Supporting information and certificates require, among other things: where held; nature and condition of track; state of weather, including wind; and certificates assuring due adherence to rules and standards by four timekeepers—the starter, the track measurers, the referee and the secretary. A special note, which has every word underlined, states:

> The track should measure 400 metres at a distance of 30 cm. from the inner edge, but owing to the difficulty of making this measurement, the measurement may be

made along the inner edge (kerb) of the track so that the tape may be pulled to a tension of 10 lb. The length of the inner kerb must not be less than 398.117 metres. Two independent measurements must be made, differing by not more than 0.13 metres.

In addition printed cardboard forms with individually numbered lap times must be submitted to the RRC for verification. It is not that the RRC assumes that cheating is rife; the level of integrity about such things in the ultraworld is ludicrously high. But there is room for carelessness, ignorance and just plain mistakes. It is easy enough to miscount laps for a dozen runners, when each one will log about 500–600 laps on a quarter-mile track. Too, a slight mismeasurement, which is relatively insignificant for a shorter race, is greatly compounded over a hundred miles.

Not only is it unfair to allow new, unverifiable records to displace the legitimate achievements of earlier runners, accurate measurement avoids forever afterward what I might dub the "short course syndrome," that bit of eyebrow raising among one's mates when they hear of an unprecedentedly fast time and question the accuracy of the course measurement. Also, the only way to measure improvement is by knowing that the mileage was right. It sounds easy enough once you know that car odometers are notoriously unreliable (because car manufacturers want less mileage to appear than should), or if you know the subtleties of calibrating a course with bicycles after taking into account ambient air temperature and the pressure of the tires, et cetera, et cetera. Particularly in the States, there have been a few "soft" as well as overlong courses. Nobody likes this, least of all the runners.

On the other hand, there is no worldwide consensus about the list the British maintain. Results from Europe, for example, appear in the magazine *Spiridon* and then are sometimes summarized in the British RRC *Newsletter* roundup of ultra events. But some of Park Barner's massive efforts in the 24-hour field will most likely always remain unofficial. Not for a minute does anyone suspect Barner or the officials of any intentional error, but they cannot meet British specs either. Since there is no official worldwide supervising body for ultrarunning, being on or off the English list—or anybody else's—only matters so much as a particular runner cares about it. Certainly in the States, Barner and anyone else is granted without question every foot that is claimed.

Not every country harbors a tiny hotbed of ultrarunners. Most

Ultrarunners from Europe, Scandinavia, and America have descended on this tiny market town in France for a 100-kilometer footrace.

of Africa, Asia and Latin America remains benignly indifferent to long-distance running. Countries that stage ultras include South Africa, the United States, England, Denmark, Finland and a number of other European countries including France, Holland, Switzerland, Belgium, Germany and Italy. The largest fields—up to as many as several thousand men and women—are found in the 100-kilometer races, which have such appeal to the metric-minded Europeans, and in South Africa's Comrades Marathon which is actually a 54-mile race.

More commonly there will be several hundred starters in the 100-kilo races, where the fields are an easy mixture of both the intensely competitive runners and the more relaxed hybrid breed who fill out the rest of the pack. These slower pedestrians mix in both running and walking, and sometimes need the full measure of the wonderfully generous time limits that might extend as long as 24 hours for a 62.1-mile course (100 kilometers). The emphasis is on making room for every ability, and there are no sneers for the tardy.

English ultraracing stands in sharp contrast, where the exclusive men's club of ultra enthusiasts is not notably sympathetic to the slow. In one 100-kilometer race at a London track, the time limit of eight hours was imposed and all those on the track—including one or two quite close to the cutoff—were encouraged to resign from the race. All the same, most European countries only feature a couple of ultra events per year, while both France and Germany sponsor four or five in the same period of time. It is impossible to know with certainty just how many occur in a year. In England, for example, there are a number of rambles and walks over national hiking trails that may go as long as 100 miles in a low-key and essentially noncompetitive fashion, but which several runners may run through simply to see what they can do.

The character of some of the European ultraraces can be quite charming, with a style and panache not found elsewhere. In late April of 1979 I jumped off a passenger train that had brought me down from Paris to the valley of the Dordogne River in south-western France. It was just dawn in the tiny market town of Belvès, and as the train slipped away I and a few other passengers hoisted our suitcases in hand and trudged up the steep hill to the center of town. They turned out, of course, to be entrants in the 100-kilometer race scheduled for the next day.

One man was a Belgian, difficult to understand, but apparently one of those gypsy souls to be found in the ultraworld who goes to every race he can. He was an odd fellow, though friendly enough;

he cut quite a figure sucking on his pipe with his remarkable bow legs, making him resemble nothing so much as a droll blue pretzel. There was also a young married couple from Paris, Robert LeBrun and his Japanese wife Reiko, both of whom had run respectable marathon times and a few ultraraces and were down to run as well as they could—not expecting to be up with the leaders but ready for a hard day's work.

As the stout and sleepy pair who ran the local café prepared my *café au lait* and croissants, I looked about at the pictures of the local rugby team on the wall, for they were clearly adored as provincial heroes. A black dog wandered in for a pat and out again. Later additions to the foreigners included Martin Thompson, an Australian medical researcher studying in London, two Englishmen, and a beaming German named Hans who spoke not a single word of French, English or Spanish.

The next day one of the few streets that ran through the town of old stone dwellings was designated as the start, and a flag for each country represented was hung from a wire stretched overhead. Although I had explained that I was in France as part of a 'round-the-world scout to look at ultrarunning, people simply treated me as if I had come all the way from New York just to run their race. Dr. Michel Carcenac and his wife had prepared a dinner for some of the foreign runners the night before, and one of their sons volunteered quite happily to accompany me on a bicycle as my second—a great relief since I knew how much it would help not to have to rely on the limited number of water stations. I was doing some stretching against the wall of the local school when I suddenly noticed seven bright-eyed schoolboys intently mimicking my stretch. Braced against the hostility I would have expected from children that age in Manhattan, I waited for the sneers that never came. Soon we were in conversation and they struggled most politely to understand my French, explaining that their teacher would not allow them to run more than 25 kilometers, since they were only about ten years old. We wished each other luck, and then the call to get ready was passed along.

There were 473 of us lined up at two in the afternoon when the gun went off. We plunged down the three kilometers of breakneck hill that the town is perched upon into the relative flat of the valley road. When a large white "10" painted on the asphalt road flashed underfoot, I asked Thompson if that could mean 10 kilometers had gone by, and he said definitely not, it was too soon. I looked at my watch and agreed. But when the large "20" and "30" came by in their turn and I finally realized just how fast I

This annual 100-kilometer race in France winds past the Dordogne River.

A Frenchman and an Englishman share the road during the 1979 Belvès 100-kilometer race.

was going, I eased off a fair amount. The course wound along the placid banks of the Dordogne, taking us through small towns and beneath the shadow of the thirteenth-century French and English châteaux that are scattered like startling visions all about the hilly countryside.

The course was not only a figure-eight but a winding one, and occasionally as the lead runners went through each town and a black-powder rocket exploded to signal their passage I could see the cloud of smoke dissolving in the wind. It was the same wind that brought in an ever-darkening sky, and I wondered how my control card would hold up if it rained. (Each competitor is issued a square card which must be punched at one of five or six control points to prove there has been no sidling off on any detours.) Little groups of French natives, men and women, stood at the edge of their fields quietly watching the runners go by. A wedding party was more animated. As the guests flooded out of the tiny church and spilled into the street, one ebullient French runner dashed up to plant a kiss of congratulation on the bride's cheek, a gallantry that delighted all.

The early levity faded as the rain came in late afternoon and we found ourselves pounding up that wretched hill back into town. I was running about ninth at that point, and thought with luck I could rise in position, but it was hard to go through town and set off into the growing darkness and ever chillier rainfall. I felt sorry for the walkers who would have to endure an entire night of that weather. By the last turnaround on my way back to the finish, I moved into fourth and hoped to hold it, though I was getting tired. Neither my handler nor I had lights to guide us and the blinding shear of oncoming headlights from passing cars was unnerving. Peering behind me uneasily, my fears were at last justified when I saw a tiny strap flashlight attached probably to someone's arm flickering behind me. I pushed my pace as best I could and soon the light was no more.

With one kilometer left to go I pelted into town—but, alas, no signs of the finish were visible. I yelled in French at passersby for directions to the finish line but they stared back at me blankly. I anxiously steamed up a steep hill and saw a parking lot a few hundred meters away. At that point I looked over my shoulder and the fifth-place man was bearing straight for me, flanked on each side by a grim companion on a bicycle. In a last bit of folly I yelled at him, asking where the finish was. When he continued to give no reply but surged closer, I realized I *had* to be going in the right direction. I was also angry at not getting a response and

Daniel Lacan forges on through rain and growing
darkness for a 1979 win at Belvès, France.

determined to get vengeance. It was one of my fastest closing 100-meters ever, and it bought me a two seconds' margin in the result sheet.

Daniel Lacan, the 33-year-old winner, ran a 6:58:19 followed by Jean Le Potier, 26, in 6:59:29. Both times bore out what LeBrun had told me earlier: "The French don't like to suffer," he said. "They want to get through it as easily as possible. But perhaps that is beginning to change now." (The first year the race was held, Serge Cottereau, a well-known ultrarunner in France, covered the same distance in 7 hours and 35 minutes!)

As a last note on some of the subtle cultural differences in ultra-running in different countries—minor points of style, perhaps—was one that I found in the green pages of the sports section of a provincial newspaper the following day. French sportswriters aim for a higher effect than their English and American colleagues. The blunt realities of the roadway I had run over the previous day seemed softened when I read the opening words: "It was a sinuous, narrow and humid course that went between plowed fields and forest in the dusk of a sad spring day when the lily of the valley 'midst the ferns weeps for the sun that has fled . . ."

4.
And How We Train . . .

In the course of my own ultrarunning and during the research I did in various countries, I spoke to dozens of ultra aficionados about their training. As one might expect, it is clear that what is needed to run or race 50 miles or longer depends very much on the individual. World-beaters such as Cavin Woodward—whose gritty, breakaway go-for-broke-early style of running has made him one of the very fastest men in the world over ultra distances— trains 70 miles in a good week and 45 miles in a bad one. In his usual blithe manner, he dismisses with a shrug the run-50-miles- every-Sunday types. Cavin likes to claim that the only time he ran longer than 20 miles on a weekend workout was when he got lost—much to his regret.

A midland runner who's a bit older than Woodward is Ron Bentley, the burr-tongued Midlander who has run 161 miles, 545 yards in 24 hours for the official world's record. The week he ran the 24-hour race, he ran four hours a day—his normal training schedule—the first four days of that week and then cut back to 20 and 12 miles! Runners of all kinds of ability can run decent ultras on anything from 30 to 200 miles a week, but a lot depends on factors that are impossible to weigh in terms of relative impor- tance: innate ability; previous years of running or involvement in other sports; and mental attitude. There is generally a drift toward the notion that the more miles you cover, the better. And among many runners, the push is toward developing sheer strength and endurance, with a correspondingly lesser emphasis on speed training, although there are some shining exceptions to that gen- erality, particularly in England.

Before turning to a closer look at the psychological aspects of their species of endurance athletics, one final and perhaps insolu- ble problem ought to be mentioned. It is the question of scale. The sheer immensity of distance is not always an easy thing to comprehend. In northeast Brazil, where I lived as a Peace Corps volunteer. I discussed ultrarunning with some peasants. We were squatting under a shade tree in a corner of a field where they were about to set off to work all day. In this region people make pilgrimages on foot to religious shrines to fulfill a vow of piety—

sometimes trudging hundreds of kilometers each way, carrying a sack or a straw basket with a few clothes and supplies. A walk into market might take several hours each way as a matter of course every week. When I told them in leagues how far I ran in races (a league equals 6 kilometers), there were nods of vigorous if surprised assent. "*Ai*, that was a mouthful of dust to cover on foot!" They had a real inkling of what it might take.

At home in the U.S. as well, the reaction to such distances is gratifyingly one of dazzlement but somehow the connections are blanker. A person can drive 60 miles in an *hour*. An hour of driving *is* a long way, but driving is dreamlike and a sense of wonder is usually lacking. So many people have an imprecise sense of distance at best. How many times—against my better judgment but impelled by restlessness with fatigue in the closing stages of a race—have I called out to some pleasant-looking type along the side of the road: "How far to the finish?" They sing back confidently: "Oh, just a mile down the road." When another three bitterly won miles go by and the end is still not in sight, I resolve repeatedly never to ask again.

It's true that pain and discomfort extend internal perception of distance enormously by making it seem longer, but an ultrarunner has experienced too much cost in his feet not to respect and record precisely what any given distance requires in effort. Christine Costa, a New York City runner who has known a number of ultrarunners, once observed that ultrarunners seem to her to be generally modest, far less overtly boastful and jealous of each other's times than those who principally run marathons.

Cavin Woodward noted: "If something happens to come up about running, somebody'll turn around and say: 'Well, I wouldn't even fancy *driving* a hundred miles without stopping!' And then recently some people said: 'Well, *you* didn't do it without stopping, did you? You could stop and have a break when you felt like it, couldn't you?' I said, 'Yeah, well, you can. But you won't break the world record if you do that.'

"Obviously for the man in the street, or a bloke that's just turned to jogging—probably even more so for the joggers, because they know how hard it is to start running—the thought of running for 12 hours without stopping . . . well, sometimes it's a lot for people to be *awake* for 12 hours! People find it difficult to comprehend because there's little else that goes on for that long. You can't relate it to another sport—football lasts just 90 minutes."

Here we arrive at the crux of a profound misconception about ultrarunners. It becomes wearying to encounter so frequently the clichéd notions about distance runners, a regular conjuration of images of gaunt-faced masochists stoically enduring miles of uncomfortable training and a sort of Elysian Mysteries of torment during a race. There *is* a measure of truth to such a portrait, but as always the thing experienced seems cheapened, misunderstood and cruder when someone who never runs reacts with extravagant admiration (or a thinly veiled distaste) to an act so "compulsive." Intimate questions such as "Why do you run so far?" or "What do you think about?" can sometimes be taken about as easily as a finger in the eye. A raid on one's emotional cupboard is not to every runner's taste. So a quick answer or a joke (or a serious answer so familiar that it's become a bore) is easier to give back than a real answer which might take a half minute or half a day to express, depending on the mood.

None of this should suggest that the ultrarunner deigns to consider and explain motivation, but a straight answer is often hard to come by. It is far easier to rest secure in simply running long distances. This is done or it is not done. There is also the talking about it, but the talking will never move the feet. And this is part of its appeal perhaps—that one runs from a certain point to another so many miles, which places one this high or this low among one's peers. And the effort in doing so not only ensures the runner of a measure of good fellowship with others, but brings as an almost inevitable corollary the promise of a sound night's sleep. Thus ultrarunning can answer questions that might not otherwise have an answer.

When I set about the task of tracking down ultrarunners, I realized that for many it wouldn't be an easy thing, to lay out with precision and eloquence their feeling for what happened to them as they ran. Not freely trapped are the fleeting impressions that crowd through the mind in the thick of a race, or the odd, ruminative thoughts about the ironic frailty of so much effort for so little that is permanently tangible. God knows, it can sometimes seem strange, running all day for hour after hour as the sun rises and falls across the sky, through towns and counties and different states. And all the while everyone who sees you thinks you belong in that neighborhood, when you really come from somewhere behind you that is now irretrievably lost.

Much of the failure of runners to talk about this comes from the mere fatigue of the mind, which cannot hold in indefinite suspension for easy recall the constantly changing mixture of thoughts: the mingled exhilaration and suspense immediately before a race, encouraging the arms and shoulders to tingle; the mind's notation of the urge to urinate and the body's apologetic excretion of a few yellow drops; the sting of resolve when you shake hands with a rival and smile—and the accompanying rattle of resolves and fantasies and evil wishes; the sullen battles with yourself when the race bumps into a bad patch. All these provide a regular universe of sensation that a runner burns through, consuming energy at a tremendous rate—quite mercifully extinguished from memory by a good night's sleep. Later the runner might remember one stretch of road, forever afterward.

Even the 24-hour run when he set the world's record—and thus achieved, perhaps, the greatest ambition of his life—was for Ron Bentley, years later, a race that was not easily recalled to mind. Only as he plucked an observer's account of the race off the shelves of his bookcase, and began to read it aloud, did he begin to laugh and offer details about the long-ago event which my earlier questioning had failed to evoke. "It's funny," Bentley said, "but you forget an awful lot."

Cavin Woodward said: "I don't think I've achieved much else in life, so anything I've achieved in athletics has been great." Rob Heron, a painfully shy red-headed Scot, conveyed in the elusive, terse answers he gave, and in his coiled, intense nervousness, an indication of sheer fox-chases-rabbit pleasure. He burned quietly to beat his fellow runners, with plain, raw competitiveness of the kind you need to push your way to the front—and to survive.

The best runners all have that, one way or another. Many of their answers are deeply bound up in character; sometimes I could see personality revealed in direct and pungent coloration. "Running is an expression of character," said Jackie Mekler, the great South African ultrarunner of the 1950's. "If you watch someone running for a little while you can tell a great deal about them."

There are no sleepyheads in this ultraworld, no maundering, repressed personalities who wander vaguely outdoors for 30-mile training runs. The effort cuts lines in the faces, restores and preserves a kind of youthfulness of body, but leaves weathered eyes, hook lines of fatigue, full expressions that carry weight and decision. This wasn't always apparent to me—not until I was out running one day and glanced sidelong at a companion's face and saw the set steady indication of will. Perhaps the art of endurance is only a gift that a certain age knows how to grasp.

So there is nothing that really allows one to rest snobbishly on the assumption that a long-distance runner is better than someone else. Not a heartwarming confession to own up to, but one I've felt at times as I ran around New York City's reservoir path, thinking that I could keep on running all day long, after all the other joggers had gone home. There is a legitimate pride there, perhaps, but the dangers are apparent to Don Choi, a San Francisco mailman who has covered his route as often as not by running it—in spite of the impediment of a 35-pound mailbag slung over one shoulder.

"Whatever I do in running, it will not compensate for short-comings in other areas. I don't go around telling everybody that I'm a runner. A lot of people on the route don't know that I run, or they think I'm a jogger. I know that if I say 'a hundred miles,' they won't comprehend well. When I run, I concentrate on my running. When I deliver my mail, I deliver my mail. But I don't go around and say—it would be socially awkward—'Look, look what I've done.' I don't fool myself with that. Nobody's perfect. I have problems. In a way certain problems do get resolved in the running, but running is something for me to enjoy. Sometimes it disturbs me when other people say, 'You're a runner.' Then they categorize me."

"I run 8 to 12 miles before breakfast, sometimes 17 miles," says Gerald Parsons, 51, an English secondary-school teacher in science. "To me it sets the seal to the day, like a kind of meditation. It's not just training, it's a way of life. In the summer, I hear the dawn chorus of birds and in the winter I hear owls."

Parsons, who is short (5′ 1½″) and slight (100 pounds), wears glasses, has an intellectual face and fine hair, which has begun to recede on his high forehead. The frail appearance is deceptive. During his mid-twenties, he spent five years working as a coal face miner near Nottingham—extremely cramped, hot and strenuous work. And on holidays in Scotland and the Lake District, he is an ardent mountaineer. Parsons was delighted with his 87th-place finish at a 100-kilometer race in Europe in the spring of 1979.

"I'm no good competitively," he said. "And I know I never will be. I run for the fun of it. I enjoy the challenge of the ultra, the adventure. Things can be too easy with the comforts of modern life. I feel we need to expose our bodies to the stress of weather. I was determined to finish in spite of the rain during the night."

Ultrarunning certainly draws its share of those who relish, or at least respect, the stoicism and discipline involved. Ultrarunning can be an enforced post-graduate course in what you're composed of.

Mavis Hutchison, who is known, somewhat to her distaste, as the Galloping Granny, is a South African housewife who ran across the U.S. at the age of 53. It was a feat that stunned some of the Americans who heard about it but hardly surprised the South African public, accustomed as they were to Mavis' 100-mile runs, her appearances in the Comrades ultrarace, and her various intercity jaunts—such as running between Johannesburg and Capetown. Sitting at home in suburban Johannesburg on a quiet Saturday afternoon, while her family wandered in and out, Mavis—whose hair is a shock of white—explained in her compellingly intense but soft-spoken way what happened when she ran in her first Comrades in 1965:

"That was my first real taste of sheer discipline. It was terrible weather. It was raining and the wind was blowing. Of course before, when I'd been training, if it had rained I'd stop. That's it! *I'm* not going to get wet. It was bitterly cold that day and before the halfway mark I was frozen. And I said if I just get to the halfway mark, I'll probably make it. I managed that, and I said, please, God, just-around-the-corner sort of thing. Eventually I made it, in 10 hours and 7 minutes. My marrow bones were frozen. That was the first time I realized that you carry on. That's when I started to realize that there's more to running than just going from point A to point B. There was a mental side as well. Physically, I'd had enough, but mentally I was able to continue and endure. That's where you learn what self-discipline and endurance really are."

For some runners such tenacity may have made itself clearly apparent long before in other aspects of life, as spouses and family eagerly attest. Ultrarunning simply gives fuller range to an innate stubbornness.

Ed Dodd, a New Jersey ultra buff who teaches math—and rolls statistics of nineteenth-century races around on his tongue the way others savor sweets, had one such simple answer for the question of why.

"I've always liked doing things for as long as I could. I remember in grade school getting on a big old Schwinn bike with balloon tires and riding this course—we lived on a hill in a suburb of Philadelphia—and I would ride up and down it, and just keep on doing it and doing it and doing it until I got tired. And I'd time myself to see how fast I could do 10 laps."

All the talk about tenacity and determination raises the issue of

Mavis Hutchison, veteran of trans–U.S. run, trains
in her hometown, a Johannesburg suburb.

pain, which sometimes can be a factor in a race (or in training) and sometimes may just never come up. On any given day there is always the matter of luck in that shifting blend of inconstant factors—weather, body chemistry, mood and pace. Not everyone wants, or needs, to run a race at full blast.

Ebullient Nina Kuscsik set a new American record for women for 50 miles at the age of 38: 6 hours, 35 minutes and 54 seconds on 10 loops of the roadway course in hilly Central Park in NYC. (Sue Ellen Trapp, an American, now holds the world record for 50 miles: 6:12:12.) She averaged 7 minutes, 50 seconds per mile dodging cyclists and pedestrians who were, as usual, unaware of the occurrence of the annual Metropolitan 50. Nina said later that she had a great time the whole way, except for a light-headed spell running into a freezing rain.

Sometimes, though, the run just isn't easy and then the real testing of soul becomes critical. For once you've accepted this play as serious, then the issue of *how* to overcome, *how* to avoid slowing down, *how* to summon up the energy to chase the next man ahead dominates the tiny horizon of your efforts. In my first 50-miler in Central Park, I remember losing all sense of caution as I rode over the delicate signals—the slightly labored breathing, the twinges from sore hamstrings, the scudding breeze of November that brought a damp mist along with it—and going for broke without meaning to. I was running well, happy to be launched after the days of relative inactivity that I underwent in order to rest thoroughly. Running without a watch and relying just on feeling as a guide, I ran through the first 10 miles at close to a 6-minute pace, which—if I had continued running that way—would have established a new course record. Whatever my follies of self-delusion, I never expected that I would be capable of doing such a thing. Further, I was always most comfortable as a slower runner, sitting back in the pack in the early stages and working my way into a better position through the final half. I always felt as if it took a good 10 or 12 miles to get warmed up for such a long race. I simply didn't have the raw talent, or the background, to sustain such a pace, but the intoxication of running in what I think was third position for a while felt awfully good. The air was purer and cleaner up front there with the lead runners. High-octane ego fuel. My relaxed pronouncements about being basically noncompetitive (enjoying the racing more to see what I could pull out of myself than to beat others, etc.) were suddenly exposed as a rather fatuous misreading of myself. I can even recall the stretch of roadway where we turned as we ran from the East Side

Shapiro, Pat Burke, and Alan Kirik share the
early stages of a 60-kilometer run.

to the West Side of the park, when I began to smell the possibility of victory—if . . .

Although I was praying for the crack-up of the two runners in the lead, I was failing to notice the signs of my own impending downfall. It came soon enough, as the ever-lurking sciatica in my right leg began to send down its familiar lightning quivers. A patch of muscle in the center of the fleshy upper back part of the thigh that was always prone to cramp, began to flutter and tighten ominously. All the creakings and vibrato voices of tendons and muscles—the first signs that come before the actual pain—began to announce themselves.

The wind picked up and a cool damp day suddenly took on a penetrating chill. A flimsy tanktop seemed inadequate but I had hardly seconds to spare for a drink at the checkpoint, let alone for a warm shirt, so I pushed on. Toes suddenly went stiff with cramp. The back of my thigh slowly tightened as some wretched elf perched there swung the vise handle around and around. I adopted an increasingly choppy stride to avoid triggering that growing sense of an imminent leg cramp, but with each inch I gave up, the more I was reduced to a trot. A couple of runners went past and I realized I would never catch sight of them again. Within the space of another lap an almost blinding fatigue set in. For the first time in about 75 races I felt physically devastated. This wasn't the rapid burn-out of a 2-mile race, where you can pull yourself through the final two laps. I simply felt voided.

I remember wondering how I could possibly continue to make my legs move, when there was nothing but that immense gravity of fatigue riddling me through and through. Gary Muhrcke, an old hand at marathons and ultras, was running in the opposite direction as he did his own workout, calling out each runner's position and offering a word of cheer. When he asked me how I was doing, I said I was a goner—my legs were dead. I felt a mild touch of pride, as if to be in such a condition absolved me of having to finish. "Screw your legs," Gary said cheerfully. "Just keep going." He gave me a slap on the rear and took off.

I suppose such advice coming from someone who hadn't been through it would have been irritating. So it *was* possible to get through somehow, I thought. The price of this instance was to will forward motion, break the run into segments, urge myself from tree to lamppost to whatever, to be content with the stony diet of sheer concentration. I had to stump through the checkpoint, my ambitions to shine in the eyes of the crowd humbled and reduced. There was no rally, either, on the last lap. No physical spark to kindle into a flame of brightening speed as the finish line approached at last. All I wanted was to get there. I knew enough to realize that however bad it felt then, the stigma of not finishing would be much worse to endure and ultimately last much longer.

Well, it wasn't really so bad, I thought, a couple of minutes after stopping. The body's ability to heal at the end of a taxing effort, however superficially, is remarkable, almost hallucinatory, so that one begins to wonder if a little more could have been squeezed out here or there. And, I decided, my time and place were not *so* terrible after all. Yes, the run had been a success and perhaps I had learned a few things—for a while at any rate.

But the question of the origin of effort is something one continues to learn over and over—it comes from the drive within. That drive is linked not only to one's own self but to other selves, however much of a dilemma that may pose. Except for journey runners, who set off on long runs against the clock, ultraracers agree by their very participation in a race to measure themselves against their peers. But they cannot be too closely influenced or they betray themselves into too slow or too fast a pace.

Mike Newton, an English ultrarunner who has won a number of 100-kilometer races in Europe, is keenly aware of how the body's ability to race hard is linked to your perception of how well you're doing in relation to others.

"I always like to run to the field if I can," Newton said. "I've got a list of all the runners, and I prefer to run against the person rather than against the course. I find that's better because you forget the distance. The problem is, if your rival cuts you, you really feel it twice as hard then. Then your legs really crack. Legs are funny things. They can really be going great stuff, and then all of a sudden the guy's only got to come past you and somehow your legs tell you they're not as good as they were a hundred yards back. It's all psychological—it must be. It's just the fact that you can't match them.

"But in the 100-kilometer it doesn't mean you're not going to get them back. In one race in France, four blokes passed me and I really felt bad. I thought, oh, this is it. And you start saying, well, I might have to settle for fifth place. People feel, oh, he shouldn't settle, but I think that attitude is positive because you don't intend to drop out, which still gives you a chance of winning the race—which I did. Because dropouts never win. If you finish the course, you *must* have a chance because so much can happen."

Another determined student of ultrarunning is 38-year-old Brian Jones, whose six-foot-two-inch frame is muscular and massive.

Brian, who weighs 185 pounds, is one of the heaviest ultrarunners on the circuit, well up in Park Barner's class as one of the big men. Despite his gentle, easygoing manner, Brian's bearded face and determined stride make it amply clear that this Viking is not easily stopped. Although I needle him by suggesting that his running is a mere lumbering along, Brian's running style is as easy and pared down as the rest. Chronic leg and knee problems have caused him to plunge into a self-education course on the intricacies of lower-limb physiology and the biomechanics of running. Although he is now self-employed as a business consultant in the East Side apartment he shares with his wife Trish, a dancer, Brian has covered the full gamut of employment in earlier years. He worked selling secondhand cars, as a member of a construction crew, as a laborer on a crayfishing boat, as a diamond driller and a spell as an ecologist doing research on fish-stomach parasites. The taste for athletics goes back to schoolboy days and his time as an undergraduate at Sydney University, where he graduated in 1962 after participating in cricket, rugby, tennis and squash, in addition to a little running.

His feeling on finishing his first ultrarace a few years ago was similar to what he felt after his first marathon:

"It was a brief, euphoric instant—an incredible high. It didn't come till five minutes after I finished the ultra and it just lasted for seconds, but I felt very exhilarated. I thought it was the greatest accomplishment of my life. And I didn't have any tremendous letdown.

"Actually, two days later I decided to test myself out in endurance swimming, so I swam for six hours nonstop in a large pool. At the time I hadn't been training for swimming, but I wanted to see if the endurance would carry over. It's probably more of a mental thing—that is, in terms of lasting through them. What is it exactly? Well, it's just the same tough-minded attitude of pressing on. I've been a stoic all my life. Part of it might be that my father would get angry about something, and he could be an unforgiving person. No matter what I did I had to wait until he overcame his displeasure, until it wore off. He was big on discipline. Psychologically I had to live with that uncomfortable situation and there was nothing I could do about it.

"I remember, as a child I used to do things to excess, like practicing rugby with a friend for 4 or 5 hours. We'd keep doing it even though it had gone on past the pleasurable stage. I've always had this immoderate attitude toward leisure things—toward everything, I suppose. If I'm working on a project I'll go for 24 hours, instead of breaking it into three 8-hour portions which would probably be more productive. Maybe it's partly because I'm such a great procrastinator, so that once I'm moving I might as well take advantage of it."

When asked whether he could endure more discomfort than other people, Brian began his answer with what one hears from every long-distance road runner, no matter whether talented or not.

"I think I feel pain just the same as anyone else. Maybe I have a stronger sense of commitment than some. The only excuse for dropping out is an injury. Fatigue is not a reason. No matter how bad it gets, you can always keep on doing something. It's the commitment before the race that gets you through it—and gets you off the hook as far as a decision is concerned. Then you don't have to worry: should I continue or should I not? Feeling tired— that's just part of the game. And that fatigue is basically muscle fatigue. Mentally I'm high on drinking so much Pepsi, and it's only when I can't sleep later that I realize how hepped up I am."

During the 1978 100-miler in New York, Brian endured almost 8 hours of intense discomfort—if that is not too mild a word to use. Due to a conscious shift in running style to compensate for injuries, he over-used his thigh muscles which went dead on him at about 40 miles. I remember running past him at one point and saying hello. No answer came back from his set face as he padded onward, and I shrugged, not knowing but guessing a little at how difficult it might have been for him at the time. Recalling that period later, he said:

"You know I lost it there for a while. The finish seemed remote and I was nowhere. I had very few specific thoughts. My mind was a blank. I had just lost a sense of the beginning and the end of it all, so I just ran. It was a very specific blank feeling. I didn't hallucinate or anything. The idea of thinking seemed tremendously energy-consuming, so I never did it. I could hear what people were saying to me—but the effort to make a reply! I was at a low level. There were no waves up there. I reached a point where I just kept going till the race stopped. Maybe I'm overestimating my physical capacity that day, but it seemed that if there had been another 10 hours involved, I would have said: 'Well, so be it.' I'd reached a point where I could live with it."

The one dream that all ultra runners share is to be frictionless. Earth, air and flesh all exert drag. The sleek forward motion of a fresh day catches and bleeds against the snags that all finite things encounter. One does not run forever. Different stimuli remind you quickly enough of that. I think when I first heard of ultrarunning, part of the fascination was my notion that it must be associated with altered states of mind, or superhuman, almost Yogic-type abilities. But it is all rather ordinary after a while, and it begins out of ordinary things, stride blending into stride so rapidly and repeatedly that there is no way to differentiate one from another. At their best, the long runs are both easy and hard—easy at the start, when running seems a spontaneous ignition, and rewarding, too, when the full measure of concentration for the task at hand is required for its completion. What one takes out of it is what one is prepared to ask at the start. It may just happen to be ultrarunning, but there is no secret Masonic brotherhood of shared mystical raptures available to its devotees. That is the stuff of Sunday pulp magazines. It is enough to be on the road and launched, cut loose for a space of hours from the ordinary drag of concerns. Life can be simpler then, sometimes.

It is curious, but certainly the extravagance of monster distances teaches respect for limits. The body and the mind both need to rest. The very stubbornness that allows one to train hard must be chastened by a bad injury or a wipeout in a race. The best runners key to a fine edge—as runners at every other distance must do as well. Balance ·and restraint are as necessary as thoughtfulness, attentiveness to the clues. Ted Corbitt always mentions the ones who got too excited after a fine 100-miler and reached too rapidly, too greedily, in too short a space of time for another reward and forever afterward never ran as well again.

There is a regular universe of shadowy laws out there. Learning the long haul never ends.

Brian Jones meets the morning and a tiny
crowd after a long night of running.

Legs need help, especially during a
100-miler as Paul Soskind discovers.

3.
HOW THE
ULTRAS BEGAN

1.
The Pedestrians
and the Wobbles

I was able to reach that slightly seedy, almost forgotten section of London known as Islington by getting off at the underground station they call Angel. With the reverence of a pilgrim, I stepped out of the creaky lift that had carried myself and a small boy up the deep shaft from the tracks below to find myself in the street, gazing around already with an inflamed historical imagination. Certainly none of the shoppers who brushed by would have imagined that anything out of the ordinary had brought me to that district.

No one I asked had ever heard of the Royal Agricultural Hall, although its main entrance was just a few streets away over on Liverpool Road. As I made my way along I tried to forget the rare appearance of sunshine that April day in England, so that I could conjure up the foggy days and nights of the 1880's. The pubs and severe brick-row homes seemed much the same as they must have been then, when the hall was new.

A pity, I thought when I saw it, that the mammoth relic of the Victorian age had been abandoned to decay. The entrance was boarded up and a sign warned that dogs inside would devour any unwary visitor like myself who yearned to glimpse the splendid dimensions of the cavernous main hall—some 400 feet long by 200 feet wide, with a curved 130-foot span of roof far above the floor. For it was in this hall, 90 years earlier, that a now forgotten group of athletes called "pedestrians" set about to shatter the world's record for what is one of ultramarathoning's most extraordinary organized competitions—the 6-day (144 hours long) "go as you please" contests around an indoor track.

The men who entered these trials could walk, run, eat and sleep as they pleased on the way to toting up five or six thousand laps—which, if they had accumulated an equivalent ball of yarn, could have been unrolled from London to the northernmost reaches of Scotland. The hardy souls who began this fantastical kind of trial in the 1810's were initially heel-and-toe men—walkers, that is—until the Englishman Charles Rowell began to run sections of

The now-abandoned Royal Agricultural
Hall in London was the site
of six-day races in the Victorian era.

these races. That pragmatic breakthrough eventually led to astounding results. In 1888 at New York City's Madison Square Garden, the other major venue for 6-day races, the English "ped" George Littlewood ran 623 and ¾ miles, averaging just under 104 miles a day. Pedestrians were professional athletes who competed not only for prestige but very substantial stakes of money. For about 20 years or so, interest among the working classes was intense and the crowds, especially in the latter stages of the week, must have come up from work through the chill winter evenings to sit in the gas-lit main hall, smoking and yelling for their exhausted favorite to push on.

It all seemed a long time gone as I gazed up at the twin towers that flank the entrance doors and rise 95 feet above the street. The great belly of the arched iron and glass roof glinted in the sunlight, and the few weeds growing out of the mortar of the brick walls dipped in the breeze. Once rented out for horse shows, circuses, prayer meetings and fancy dress balls, the Agricultural Hall served in its last years as a branch of the London post office. It seemed a pity that there was no plaque, no words to commemorate the valiant—if at times comical, and even barbarous—efforts of those pedestrians.

I think it is safe to say that scarcely anyone in the world now knows in any detail what actually went on in those events. One of the foremost 6-day buffs is Peter Lovesey, an English writer whose speciality has been books about crime and about sports, particularly long-distance running. His first detective novel, *Wobble to Death*, is about the mysterious death of one of the participants in a 6-day affair, known familiarly as a "wobble," suggestive of the advanced physical decay which must have overtaken the entrants, but which might also have referred to the idiosyncratic waggle of tired walkers who had to conform to the still current rules of form. Walking, by the by, is as demanding a sport as running, however fewer its adherents may be and however comical it may look to the uninitiated.

Peter Lovesey discussed the history of ultrarunning in Britain with me in the study of his quiet home in Cheam, a London suburb. Although his lanky frame suggested a runner, past or present, Lovesey insisted that he was "just hopeless" at running as a schoolboy, and never pursued the sport further. His study was lined on one side with a sober array of books and on the other with posters of nubile Susan Anton, heroine of the movie *Golden Girl*, which is based on a book of the same title that Lovesey wrote under the pseudonym, Peter Lear.

I asked him why ultrarunning and walking first appeared in England rather than elsewhere, suggesting that perhaps it had to do with that special outlook of the British, a willingness to endure. He answered:

"I'm not sure whether it's anything particularly in the national character or whether it arises out of quite different things. Athletics were far better organized in Britain—without being too chauvinistic—than anywhere else in the world in the nineteenth century. And there was this tradition of running footmen which goes right back to the seventeenth century. The lord of the manor would say *his* footman was far better than the other bloke's at carrying messages. Then they would run against each other over quite long distances. A running man in those days was quicker than a man on horseback or a coach, because of the state of the roads. Men could travel much longer distances and were far more reliable. Later on they became the first professional athletes.

"There got to be a few traditional distances—10-mile races were the great thing in the 1700's. One man actually died an hour after setting up a record of 54½ minutes on Richmond Green. He just wasn't trained for that sort of effort. While the time may seem ludicrous nowadays, it still seems tragic, doesn't it? By modern standards, most of these people on into the nineteenth century weren't well trained. Even over the shorter distances they frequently would collapse after a race was over and be insensible for a time. These people would put tremendous efforts into their running. In terms of effort they might be doing more than the modern superathlete does to run themselves into unconsciousness. I think that's quite heroic, really."

Most of the ultra feats in the eighteenth century involved not runners but walkers, usually men, who covered distances as far as 300 to 400 miles. Hundred-mile walks in 24 hours were sometimes done on the roads or around a horse-race track, although Lovesey says there is some question as to how reliable the watches were. Around 1823 a 7-year-old girl ran for 4 hours at a time on several occasions. Another young girl in the nineteenth century apparently ran and walked 30 miles 3 times—in a little less than 8 hours on each occasion—taking wine and water for sustenance and remaining in excellent spirits throughout. A man named Captain Barclay walked 1,000 miles in 1,000 hours—covering one mile each hour. He was never able to rest very long and he had to endure abysmal weather. Thousands came to watch and Captain Barclay earned about £16,000—the equivalent today of $400,000. Clearly, there was what one might term an exceedingly thin tradition for such events, but considering how hard people worked, how different and how difficult it was to travel around, and how little was known about training, such a sprinkling of endurance events was at least a beginning.

According to Lovesey, pedestrianism was at its social heyday about 1810 when it was very much a high-class affair, but by the 1860's and the era of the Industrial Revolution it had become considerably less fashionable. The predominant sports in England now, such as cricket, rugby and soccer, hadn't yet been established on a regular basis, so pedestrianism had a large following among the working class in the big cities, each of which had its own track for such events.

The earliest 6-day race apparently took place about 1875, and soon the colorful, dynamic figure of Sir John Astley, sports promoter par excellence, dominated the scene. At one time a bit of a runner himself, as well as a Member of Parliament, he set up a championship belt and money prizes to encourage interest and organized races both in London and New York. Both the grander and lesser lights who actually hoofed around the tracks under Sir John's auspices were a varied lot. One "Corkey," whose Christian name was William Gentleman, was a one-time record holder who was described by Sir John in his autobiography, *Fifty Years of My Life*, as "a very quaint-looking old chap of 46 . . . had a peculiar high action. He didn't look a bit like staying, was as thin as a rail and stuttered very funnily, but in Mrs. Corkey he possessed a real treasure. She never left him day or night and was always ready to hand her sweetheart a basin of delicious and greasy eel-broth, that he loved so well, and which obviously agreed so famously with him." Henry "Blower" Brown, also a record holder, who had been a brickmaker, had "early distinguished himself by the rapid manner he trundled his barrel of bricks to the kiln and back again for another load and like all brickmakers he was wonderfully fond of beer. Therefore when old Jack Smith wished to get an extra spurt out of his protégé he used to yell at him on the track with the same exhortation and promise whenever his instinct told him it was needed: 'Well done, Blower. Go to it, Blower. You've got 'em all beat, my beauty. Yes, Blower shall have a barrel of beer all to himself if he wins. Go to it, Blower.' One day Blower showed signs of shutting up and as he was more animal than angel, Smith and I agreed that it would be a good thing to wake him up a bit by putting him in a bath, quite a new sensation for him. So we took him to my lodgings hard by, and I ordered two chops to be got ready for him and then put him into a hip bath of real hot water which livened him up considerably, fairly making him sing out. When we got him nicely dry, the chops appeared. At last I was helping Blower into his running suit, I was horrified to observe old Smith busily employed gobbling up all the best parts of the chops, leaving only the bone, gristle and fat. When I expostulated with him on his greediness and cruelty to his man, he replied: 'Bless yer, Colonel, Blower has never had the chance of eating the inside, he likes the outside.' And sure enough, the brickmaker cleaned up the dish, with the result that he won first prize, doing 542 miles, a grand performance, and what is more, his appetite and thirst were in no way impaired."

Several other men were quite extraordinary for their persistence, talent and longevity in the sport. Edward Payson Weston, a Rhode Islander, originally a news vendor on a railway, walked from Boston to Washington, D.C., in order to get to Lincoln's inauguration in 1861. He was then just 21 years of age. Although he arrived late after his 443-mile trek he drew an enormous amount of attention. Six years later he walked over 1,300 miles from Portland, Maine, to Chicago, in 26 days. Forty years later he did it again, bettering his time over the first trip by 29 hours. In 1874 at Madison Square Garden he tried in May, September and October to become the first walker to break 500 miles in 6 days but got no further than 436 miles on his third attempt. In December he tried it in Newark, New Jersey, and made it with 26 minutes to spare.

Dan O'Leary, who was seven years Weston's junior and a little heavier although they were both the same height (5' 8") emigrated to the States when he was 20 years old. He sold books and pictures on installments to the poor of Chicago. His athletic career led to a changed and more prosperous life—he was to cross the Atlantic 44 times in pursuit of world records and long-standing rivals like Weston. In addition to holding the world record for a time, his career best was a 525-mile wobble in 1880 in San Francisco. Years of competition did not interfere with his friendship with Weston, and when O'Leary was 50 years old he walked 2,500 miles across America with Weston in 9 weeks. O'Leary celebrated his *81st* birthday by walking 100 miles to win a $100 bet.

Much as Sir John Astley enjoyed the success of American ultrawalkers, he looked around restlessly at the close of the 1870's for a local lad who could win back the championship belt from O'Leary. Charles Rowell, a boat boy at the Guards Club in Maidenhead, showed some promise as a runner and was promptly taken under Sir John's sponsorship. Rowell, then in his early twenties, "a very clean made, muscular young fellow," was to revolutionize the wobbles by introducing longer and longer spells of running. Since the other peds kept in shape by frequent competitions, Rowell set about training with a vengeance. He ran on a treadmill to strengthen his legs, dashing along the towpath following the Cambridge crew shells as they were out training on the river. Rowell sometimes ran up to London one day and back the next—60 miles each way in under eight hours, still impressive training of a kind that very few ultrarunners ever do nowadays. In Rowell's first wobble in New York City in March 1879, he earned back the belt and was $20,000 richer, a very considerable sum in those days. He lost to Weston in London that summer but in New York again in the fall he won and earned himself another $30,000.

Such sums of money—in addition to the public adulation—did much to encourage a number of men to try their hand at such things. It must have been intoxicating in spite of the grinding tedium to be occasionally pelted with flowers and presented with six-foot-high horseshoe flower bouquets. Rowell, flush with his earnings, took three trotting horses back to his newly acquired farm in England. On his return the reporters went straight to Charles Rowell first, ignoring the disembarking actors and politicians. Sadly, when Rowell died almost three decades later he had lost all his wealth and was living in poverty. (He was not the only pedestrian who came atangle with fortune. George Hazael, a fellow countryman and for a while world champion who made "barrels of money," was later reduced to the hard life of a bottle-and-scrap-iron peddler.)

Charles Rowell was undoubtedly one of the most remarkable men to ever circle those tiny tracks. At the end of February 1882, he participated in his last race in New York. In a little-known monograph entitled "Six-Day Races," Tom Osler and Ed Dodd (themselves ultrarunners from New Jersey) described Rowell's intentions and achievements on that occasion:

"He intended to make it memorable by establishing an unbreakable world record. He almost succeeded. His first three days saw the following:

100 miles—13:26:30
200 miles—35:09:28
24 hours—150 miles 395 yards
48 hours—258 miles 220 yards
72 hours—353 miles 220 yards

"Of these marks, only the 100 miles and 24 hours have been bettered today. Rowell proved by these marks that he was the greatest ultramarathoner of all time. Even today the world record for 24 hours is only 11 miles further than Rowell's 1882 mark, and Rowell faced another five days of running!

"At the close of the third day, poor Rowell accidentally gulped down a cup of warm vinegar. His stomach became sick and he retired from the race on the fifth day. George Hazael won with a new world record of 600 miles 220 yards."

There are a number of interesting sidelights on these 6-day affairs. For one thing, there were frequently two separate tracks set up in the same arena. The inside track was the domain of the better, higher status competitors, while the outer track was for the less experienced ordinary working men who, as Lovesey suggests, "probably came in off the streets and thought they might make a little money by trying to walk around the thing for a few days." The reason for this isolation of the separate tracks, he suggested, was to avoid any possible interference, since a certain amount of hacking and kicking went on.

"You see, one thing about professional athletics that you can argue in its favor *is* accuracy. There was a lot of money at stake and I think the people who were betting would have wanted a pretty strong assurance that the distance was accurate. The track was measured with a sort of surveyor's wheel before the start, usually in the presence of the crowd. I can see that the system of lap scoring could have been confusing and lead to all sorts of mismanagement. But for these major events, it was probably reliable. And the way the record was edged up from a little more than 500 miles steadily to 623-odd miles is the way records improve nowadays. As for how much running they did, they did quite a bit sometimes but you can't be sure from the accounts just how much."

The reason for the races being 6 instead of 5 or 7 days, Lovesey added, was that in Victorian England Sunday was a strictly observed day of rest. Therefore a race had to be sandwiched in between two Sundays. Hence, the races began early Monday morning about 1:00 a.m. and finished around 10:30 or 11:00 the following Saturday night. Sunday-morning judges and participants alike were reverently seated in church.

In the mid-1880's, the wobbles plummeted in popularity, although a brief renaissance took root for some reason or another in Philadelphia from 1899 to 1903. Six were held in the space of one year. Sir Astley's weakness for gambling led to his getting

MONDAY SEPT 6th
TILL SATURDAY SEPT 11th
G. MASON
C. THOMAS
H. MUNDIN
W. SMITH
W. FRANKS
J. DEAN
H. KING

The longest regular foot races ever held, "wobbles," began in England in the 1880's.

"skinned" and he was no longer able to promote the races as he had in the past.

"Another reason was that cycling was beginning to come in," Lovesey said. "Cycling had more to offer the spectators and the gamblers, since there was more change of fortune. Maybe people began to suspect in the later eighties that the races were fixed so that certain people would be allowed to win. There were various permutations on the six-day contest, and it went on in one form or another until well into the pre–World War One period."

Certainly their gradual disappearance from the sporting scene must have greatly satisfied newspaper correspondents and editorial writers, who were dubious about their value. Witness this concluding paragraph from the *Illustrated London News*, 9 November 1878:

> *We cannot take leave of the subject without expressing an earnest hope that we have seen the last of these painful struggles against nature. It may be an advantage to know that a man can travel 520 miles in 138 hours, and manage to live through a week with an infinitesimal amount of rest, though we fail to perceive that anyone could possibly be placed in a position where his ability in this respect would be of real use to him . . . So, what is to be gained by a constant repetition of the feat? As long, however, as prizes are offered, so long will men come forward to compete for them; and we suppose the public will continue to flock to these races until a man dies upon the track. Then there will be a sudden revulsion of feeling, a howl of virtuous indignation, and such exhibitions will be sternly repressed. But why not repress them before anything so serious has occurred? We have no hesitation in stating that prize-fighting is mild and humane, compared with such sport [!] as six-day races; and that the one should be rigidly put down and the other encouraged, in the same country, is a gross and glaring inconsistency.*

There had been scenes of brutality on the track, one of the more notable taking place in 1884 in New York when Patrick Fitzgerald was racing against Charles Rowell. Fitzgerald's slim lead over his opponent grew slimmer during the last day. In desperation his handlers had him bled by making incisions in his thighs to reduce the stiffness.

"It worked," the two authors noted dryly, "and Fitzgerald staggered to a new world record of 610 miles." It was also the end of Fitzgerald's running career. His weight shot up in four years from 160 to 240 pounds. During George Littlewood's 623-mile-plus effort at Madison Square Garden in 1888, he retired briefly from the track and was reposing in an alcohol bath when someone dropped a match in, burning him rather badly. But he still finished the race, in spite of the injury one of his feet sustained. One American journalist who witnessed some of these affairs took pity on "the poor, jaded, abused bodies" of the runners and said not only did they make him sick, but the memory of them would play havoc with his sleeping hours for days to come. There was even a bill introduced in the Pennsylvania legislature to outlaw the sport entirely.

As for Edward P. Weston, that "Yankee of extraordinary staying powers," his career as a pedestrian outlasted the decline of the wobbles. In 1909, when he was 70, he walked from New York to San Francisco, and the next year walked from Los Angeles to New York, averaging 37 miles a day the first trip and 46 miles daily the second time around. At the age of 74 he legged it from New York to Minneapolis. Two years before his death at the age of 90, he was struck by a cab and left partially paralyzed. His comrade, O'Leary, died at the age of 88.

During all this flurry of dramatic activity in the last thirty years of the past century, ultrarunning in a quiet way finally began to come of age.

Andy Milroy, a schoolteacher who lives in the quiet rural town of Trowbridge in the English county of Wiltshire, is another remarkable ultra buff who breathes statistics. His passion led to the publication of the authoritative mimeographed publication entitled: "Distance Running Progressive Bests." This thin booklet lists each of the record holders since the nineteenth century for various events: 50 miles, 100 kilometers, 24 hours, and so on through the usual litany. In a brief foreword, Milroy explains why most of the records begin in the 1870's and 1880's. The running footmen of the 1600's, he notes, gave rise to professional pedestrians.

By the eighteenth century races were frequent but they were run on roads, between milestones, or on racecourses. Measurement of distances was inconsistent. It was not until the early 1850's that accurately measured circular running paths began to appear. The means of

*timing improved as well. In 1855 a watch with an inde-
pendent second hand was invented, enabling events to
be timed to ¼, or even ⅕ of a second . . . Records had
been established by the early 1860's and there were
professional athletes specializing in track distance running.*

Further, the growth of amateur "athletics," as track and field
are referred to in England, began to take hold in the 1860's. The
British Amateur Athletic Union began to recognize distances from
10 to 50 miles as legitimate for record attempts. Surely, there
were some simple human dynamics at work as well. Word gets
around among men who had a taste for trying such things that
someone might have run such and such a time under the auspices
of a certain pub, or for a running club. A chance to earn a few
pounds, or the simple factor of competitiveness, most likely
explained the occasional attempts at those difficult distances. And
surely the 6-day affairs must have been an added stimulus—for
one thing, to run 50 miles must not have seemed quite so terrible
or beyond one's own capacities when compared with the distances
regularly posted at the Islington Hall.

In 1879, a Mr. F. W. Firminger, an Englishman, ran 50 miles
in 6 hours, 38 minutes and 41 seconds at the Stamford Bridge
track. Five years later John Fowler-Dixon, who later appeared at
ultra record attempts when he was much older to cheer on the
new generation, took almost 18 minutes off the time. Just a year
later he improved on the time yet again. In 1913, Edgar Lloyd,
another runner who became one of the grand old men of English
ultrarunning, set up a time of 6:13:58 at Stamford Bridge, a
record that was to stand for almost 40 years! The 50-mile track
record moved into the 5-hour range then and remained there
from 1952 until 1975, when Cavin Woodward ran a 4:58:33 at
the Tipton track, doing better than 6 minutes per mile. The
current record of 4:53:28, held at present by Don Ritchie, is
about the equivalent of a 5:50-per-mile pace.

It is only fair to note here several factors. Records are kept for
track runs only, since road courses are not so consistently reliable
if one is keeping records from around the world, and not so easily
compared one to another. The downhill and uphill combinations,
as well as the differences between running on a concrete, dirt or
asphalt surface, can considerably affect the effort and strain involved in any given race. Of course, track records are more than
bland statistics that reflect the very best that might be expected.

The sometimes rain-soaked cinder tracks of England are very different to struggle through than the equally difficult problem of coping with a tropical sun and oceanside humidity at the track belonging to the Savages running club in Durban, South Africa. So, too, the now-forgotten track records set up by Jackie Mekler and Wally Hayward at 6,000 feet above sea level in Johannesburg, where the thin air puts more stress on the oxygen-carrying capacity of runners.

You have only to glance at the old photographs hung up in the clubhouses, now turned brown from age, or leaf through the works of the illustrated artists who sketched these events, to realize how very different a world it was a hundred years ago. The heavy leather shoes; the knee-and-elbow-length running costumes that more nearly resemble antique bathing costumes than track suits suited for easy action of arms and legs; the smoke-filled arenas—such inconveniences must have hampered performance, to say nothing of the welter of odd training fashions and costumes that flourished in those days.

Some of the conventional wisdoms seem to have survived unaltered from the time of the Greeks—both good and bad. It is not quite so simple as casting a sigh of pity for such benighted ways. Even today's runners might learn a little from early examples. There was a generally popular reliance on meat as a source of energy, although it is now well established that carbohydrates figure as a much more fundamental and ongoing source of energy during a run. For the most part there was a very firm mistrust of imbibing water or other liquids during runs—needless to say a hazardous and stressful condition for any athlete to undergo, particularly in hot weather. Other areas are a little cloudier in terms of their pernicious effects. Smoking cigarettes and cigars occasionally was not viewed as being particularly harmful, and it is interesting to note that Cavin Woodward will sometimes puff on a cigarette to relax. And in spite of the warnings in U.S. running magazines about the effect of alcohol or heavily sugared and salted diets, the English and South Africans are great beer and ale drinkers. The English in particular have a yen for sweets and cakes and sugared goodies that is never slaked.

Diet is always a matter of controversy and I hardly mean to explicate at this point my own little nest of notions on the subject. It is simply refreshing to see how differently ultrarunners from that distant Victorian generation down through ours have handled themselves. The long-dead Len Hurst (he passed away in 1937 at the age of 66) was one of the record holders on the London-

Brighton course. His 1903 time held up for 21 years until the exceptional Arthur Newton came along. Hurst had great abilities: when he was 22 he ran 183 miles in 30 hours, and at the age of 24 he ran 151 miles to win a 20-hour race, a truly exceptional feat. He was fond of occasional mustard baths and massage. He liked to drink a pint of bitter ale before eating, claiming that it aided his digestion. He also imbibed egg-and-sherry concoctions during competition. Today's ultrarunners have sometimes taken a nip of one potent drink or another (usually with great discretion) and swear by the swift kick onward it gave them.

In America, for some reason, massage is not nearly so highly regarded as abroad, although this old accompaniment to very long races probably can be extremely beneficial. Yet Americans have shown much greater interest in stretching exercises before and after runs than their foreign colleagues, although this is slowly changing. Both Jackie Mekler and Wally Hayward, two of South Africa's greatest megarunners, told me that one of the things they now consider most important for longevity in running is a good stretching program.

A final notation on the differences in conditions between ultrarunners in the last century and in the more recent part of this one, has a peculiarly apt significance—stemming from what one might call the blazed-trail mentality. Most people take as a goal what everyone else around them believes in as well. They follow the markings of whomever has gone along before them in the forest, and they go just that far. If they are ambitious they look a little beyond and cut out for themselves another bit of trail. Most records in ultrarunning improve in small steps, and in spite of all the gradual improvement in training and running gear I cannot help wondering if to some degree—not a measurable kind of thing at all—runners think that at best they can improve on a record very slightly and so aim for the slight improvement. There is a kind of confidence one can have, knowing that 100 miles in 12 hours has been done by one or two other men—ah, if they could, we think, then maybe we can move along a little faster. There is for many, although not all, a gradual increase in self-assurance as longer and longer distances are completed at faster and faster speeds. The very best runners often experience changes when they begin to win races, or at least to hold up at the top of an international pack. Then, suddenly, their own times begin to come down as they realize they don't need to back off from the cutting edge and that they can sustain more than they thought, can *be* better runners than they ever imagined. It is not merely the miles and miles' worth of ever mightier muscle mitochondria and glycogen deposits in the legs, but a connection that links body to mind and heart. Optimism and hope about his or her ability is what guides the runner on to his very best achievements.

Jackie Mekler of South Africa once put it this way: you must think positively and clearly with every step of a race. Let go of that inspired focus, he suggests, and you will falter both mentally and physically. Not only does this apply to one's personal development I believe, but to the development of every generation of runners that comes along. It is perhaps why so much variation in training and coaches leads to excellent results in different ways. Belief in the rightness of the preparation matters at least as much as the actual thing done—perhaps.

There is a Sufi story told about a man who learned to walk on water but accidentally used the wrong chant to do so—"wrong" mantra but right belief therefore bringing about a stunning result. Which leads me to say that I hope that the current generation of ultrarunners—or any that follows—doesn't develop a subtle disdain for the slower efforts of their predecessors. Even if future running times cease to improve because of the finite improvability of the human body in relation to given laws of mass, gravity and energy—even then, would it not be most generous and realistic to judge the past in terms of effort expended?

Not a great deal happened in the world of ultras after the 1880's. About 40 years passed with little that is noteworthy occurring. Interest in the standard marathon (26.2 miles) flourished and perhaps some of the professional money then available drew off younger, talented runners. The next significant surge of interest took place 11,000 miles to the south of England in South Africa. Once again it was the energy and push of a determined race organizer that provided a forum for a great physical challenge.

The inspiration came to Vic Clapham, a veteran of the East African campaign during World War I. Clapham, an engineer for the South African railways, was not an athlete himself but he came up with an idea whose ultimate popularity and influence he could hardly have imagined. In an account he wrote some time afterward, he recalled the origin of his idea:

It was during those terrible days in 1918, and our "boys" had done some wonderful work, that I attended a meeting of the First Returned Soldiers' Organization, and it was at this meeting that it struck me that the objects of this great league should include the fostering of the sporting spirit with the British Empire.

Rudyard Kipling's sneer came into my mind. He referred to the young Britisher either as a "muddled oaf" or as a "flanneled fool." This same "average Britisher" was then (1918) showing, surely, of what stuff he was made, and proving up to the hilt that the sports grounds of the British Empire were the training grounds for soldiers.

The London to Brighton Stock Exchange walk came into the train of my thoughts, and I asked myself, "Why not a place-to-place event for South Africa?" and this led me to the idea of a race from Durban to Maritzburg (also called Pietermaritzburg).

I then thought that perhaps this was too strenuous but when I remembered some of the nightmare marches of 25 miles at a stretch in East Africa on starvation rations, vermin-ridden, badly clothed, and unwashed, and carrying a kit of anything up to 90 lbs., and this often done with a high temperature or with malaria or dysentery, I thought that the 54 miles from Durban to the City would be light, comparatively, especially as the competitors had a prize to go for, were in splendid health, were in light attire, used to the best of nourishment, and possessed of a knowledge that they might retire without being made a maul of by some stray lion.

... The wonderful response to the call for prizes, the magnificent entry list gives one heart to carry on, just as the "boys" carried on "on the fields of Flanders, on the sands of Egypt," and in the bush of East Africa.

... May South Africa in the future breed such men as she has done in the past—stickers every one!

Well, it was glorious and heartfelt rhetoric, but Clapham met a cool response initially. The name "the Comrades Marathon" refers to the Comrades of the Great War, comprised mostly of veteran foot soldiers. The first one took place in May 1921, and the races have continued every year since with the exception of four years during World War II, making the Comrades for all practical purposes the oldest continuous ultrarace in the world. In 1921, 34 men lined up for the gun and exactly half that number finished the long and dusty route. It was not until the following year, with a field of 89 ready to make a go of it, that one of ultrarunning's most influential personalities appeared.

Arthur F. H. Newton, the bespectacled, mild-mannered farmer who grew prize-winning tobacco and cotton, came down to the race with a burning grievance in his heart. His farm had been brought to the edge of bankruptcy, Newton felt, through being situated in the middle of a native area. Newton owned 1,350 acres of Crown Land in a remote district of the province of Natal, which he started clearing and planting in 1911. His farming career was interrupted by World War I, in which he served as a motorcycle dispatch rider. From 1918 to 1921 he tangled with the local natives over their refusal to dip their cattle in a tank to prevent tick disease; over long-due back rent from sharecroppers who lived on his land; and over their refusal to provide work gangs to help at harvest time. Goaded by the government's refusal to allow him to exchange his land for a similar tract in white territory, or to offer adequate recompensation, Newton decided that "any man who made a really notable name of such [amateur athletics] would always be given a hearing by the government."

Newton's tenacity as a farmer transferred well to sport. Beneath his mild, reserved exterior was a very determined man. Although his experience in running and racing was limited he began serious training in January 1921. Scarcely five months later he was still an unknown. One of the papers in that western province, *The Natal Witness*, printed the following account:

> *Fully a couple of thousand people turned out in the dark at Toll Gate, Durban, to witness the start . . . Hundreds of motor cars and cycles were also traveling backwards and forwards along the route, and at every wayside inn and private dwelling house crowds congregated to give the runners as they passed a hearty cheer and provide anything required in the line of light refreshments. As a matter of fact, several who are continually on the road interested in various cycle races, etc., . . . state that they have never witnessed such enthusiasm and such a lot of picnic parties and spectators on the road as they witnessed during this race.*

Later, the correspondent arrived at Pietermaritzburg to watch the finish.

It was 2:40, when a flutter of excitement and a sudden acceleration of people showed that the great moment had arrived. There had been quite a crowd before, but in a few seconds swarms of Europeans, Indians and Natives seemed to materialize from the very air, and one wondered how the runner would be able to cut his way through.

One caught a glimpse of him as he battled past the Police Station. Here is a light running impression:— A young fair man, very like the British Army officer type, red as a turkey cock from the sun and sweat, smiling faintly at the roars of cheers going up to encourage him. Looking as if sorely tried, yet sure to finish, a man who had actually conquered the physical exhaustion that ought to have beaten him ages ago, one who was indeed demonstrating the power of mind over matter.

They say Newton had run all the way, not stopping for a second to rest or for a massage. There did appear to be the set speed of the automaton about his movements, as if he had sworn to run at a certain mechanical gait till he got to his goal.

Newton took 8 hours and 40 minutes to complete the course—which would have earned him 1,038th place in the 1979 "up" run. From the beginning, the start has usually alternated between the city halls in the respective cities. The run from the shore of the Indian Ocean covers a tremendous amount of climbing, although the so-called "down" course from Maritzburg to Durban has very long hilly stretches as well. Newton, who was then 39 years old, was shouldered by the crowd.

His friends "eventually got him away to less exciting quarters than the dressing room, and after he had been caught again by the camera man he was kidnapped by the ladies, who entertained him to tea far from the madding crowd."

It is easy to imagine Newton's painfully mixed feelings at his victory, for he later referred to his victory lap around the track at the Show Ground as "appallingly embarrassing." Newton said that his Comrades victory might be his last appearance on the road. Clearly he had little idea of how he was to inspire and rally the coming generations of would-be ultra artists, through personal example and advice offered over pots of tea and plates of cake. At the time his thoughts were on his parents; he was sure they'd be pleased at the news of his win.

The controversy over his farm dragged on, so the following year found Newton back for a second try at Comrades. In the intervening 12 months he covered more than 9,000 miles in training, which averages out to over 170 miles a week! Newton was running a little less than a marathon in training every day which, by the current standards—nonexistent as they were for ultrarunners at that point—was simply phenomenal. The softness of the 1921 time was apparent when Newton trimmed it down by more than two hours, taking a little less than 7 hours to complete the course, 52 minutes ahead of the second-place finisher. So much ahead of his expected arrival did the dusty Newton arrive that only by a last-minute scamper were officials able to get a clock on him at the finish. Because he'd had so much time to devote to his training while his competitors had not—Newton was no longer farming—he refused the first prize of a handsome timepiece, which he had "installed in the office of the Town Clerk of Harding, Natal, whose populace he had found so encouraging." Newton then decided that he was ready for a try at the world record for 50 miles.

2.
Women Also Ran

The 1923 Comrades was remarkable as well for the meteoric appearance of ultrarunning's first woman runner in modern times, a Miss Frances Hayward. The 2,000 spectators at the start kept asking: "Where is the lady?" until at last she appeared, wearing "a businesslike green gymnasium uniform." *The Natal Witness* account continues: "Miss Hayward made a steady pace, dropping to a walk on the hills and at Thorneybush she was last but one, a good mile behind the others. She looked cheerful and fit."

If her entry had been official Miss Hayward would have finished 28th among the eventual 31 finishers (there were 37 dropouts), but her official entry was canceled although officials did not discourage her appearance. It was the same conservative attitude by male officials around the world that continues to absurdly misread women's capabilities right up to the present day. (Women were not permitted to run Comrades officially until 1975.) The press and the public cared little for such niceties, however, and her time of 11:35:00 was widely praised:

> *In finishing the course in well under the stipulated 12 hours, she accomplished a very fine feat indeed, and one that reflects great credit on her powers of endurance. She did what over 38 men in the race failed to perform, and the champions of women's equality will no doubt extract great satisfaction from that fact. Miss Hayward walked a good deal of the way, but she finished well and something should be said of the magnificent reception she received from the people of Durban ... The streets were packed with people all anxious to catch a glimpse of this plucky little girl.*
>
> *The crowd, numbering thousands, literally swamped her, and it was only by the aid of a mounted constable that she was able to reach Lords at all, whilst the cheering and the noise were deafening ... A word is also due to F. W. Rodgers, who ran with her all the*

way from Maritzburg to Durban, and coached her
through. The two finished in a dead heat at Lords,
and the sporting manner in which Rodgers stuck to
his partner was certainly fine.

A few more details have survived about this woman pioneer. She wore specially made shoes of leather with suede tops, and had warm tea and oranges for sustenance along the route. Although she loved golf, tennis and swimming, long walks fascinated Miss Hayward and she trained for Comrades for three months, doing 8 miles every day and 26 on Sundays. It isn't clear whether she walked, or ran, or combined the two in her jaunts.

"Now that I have done it," she said in an interview after the race, "I think it is too much. It is the last 10 miles that kill. I personally feel quite fit and should have no hesitation in taking part in a 44-mile run."

She was asked whether a 44-miler would attract other women runners.

"Oh, yes, I am sure of it," she replied. "I have been informed that when my entry was announced there were eight applications for my address from girls who expressed a desire to train with me."

Since 1923 when Frances Hayward donned her green jumper to run in South Africa's Comrades race, few women have followed her example, until very recently. The reasons are so obvious as to hardly bear enumeration. Clearly expectation, myth and lack of opportunity had an immense amount to do with it. Innate physical limitations that would make it dangerous or difficult for women to carry off long distances simply do not exist. All the same, in relative terms, very few women do run ultras nowadays but many of them come out about middle ground in the men's fields— or better. Undoubtedly the improvement in standards for women in ultra running will rise dramatically in the next ten years. The theory that women are better suited for long distance or ultra running because they carry extra stores of body fat has been advanced by Ernest Van Aaken, a German coach and researcher, and Joan Ullyot, a San Francisco exercise physiologist and marathoner. However recent research by David Costill, an American researcher in exercise physiology, calls their surmise into dispute and suggests that men may, in fact, burn body fats more efficiently than women.

Martin Thompson, an Australian ultrarunner who has been doing research in exercise physiology in England, says that there

Lydi Pallares, a 39-year-old mother of three, sets a
new American women's record for 100 kilometers on a hot
Miami day—9 hours 10 minutes 39 seconds.

is "nothing to suggest metabolically that Van Aaken's right on. The leanest marathon runner has enough to go from here to wherever. Extra fat would be working against male or female runners, since much of it is metabolically inert in terms of propulsion across the ground. What he and Ullyot have said is very much hypothesis, but I've heard it cited frequently. Something almost becomes unwritten law because it's stated over and over."

Regardless of whether or not the researchers come to an agreement, women are beginning to appear in ultras more and more frequently. There were over a dozen women in the 1979 Comrades 54-mile race in South Africa. And in the U.S. dozens of women have now run in ultra races. As for England, it's a sorry record of unofficial lady ghosts who detect just enough tolerance beneath the official frowns to compete, with the unwritten proviso that it just not happen too frequently. The one class event which would appeal most to women marathoners in England is the London–Brighton 55-mile race which will finally allow official women entrants for the first time in the fall of 1980.

Europe and Scandinavia have a small but apparently fairly consistent tiny minority of women ultrarunners. When we consider the very recent absurdities that took place in the roadrunning scene in the U.S. (irate officals in various states refusing to let women run in the 1960's—even in 5-mile races), the tremendous change in attitudes seems fabulous, however overdue. The long hangover about women's "frailty" dies hard, however. To this date women are still not able to run races longer than 1,500 meters in the Olympic Games. Women's ultrarunning is very much a wide open frontier, just as marathons were for women in 1970, and the comparatively soft times posted by women are beginning to tighten up. The next five or ten years are likely to see more women and far better times on the roads and tracks.

The ultra clan in the U.S., at any rate, is relaxed about the women who happen to be in the race. It's just fine if whoever wants to run, runs.

A month after the 1923 Comrades, Newton, the 41-year-old minister's son, took to the roads for what turned out to be a successful try at lowering Lloyd's 6:13:58 for 50 miles to a new time of 5:53:05. This record came in spite of its being done on a part of the hilly Comrades course (Newton did not care to run around a track because of the monotony), and apparently at first the newspapers in England refused to believe that the South African runner had done what was claimed. And the next year, to cap off an extraordinary start to a novice's running career, Newton pulled off a "hat-trick," winning three consecutive times. Not until 1968 did anyone else match that feat.

As if that were not enough, Newton won Comrades for the fourth consecutive time in 1925. In 1926, following a last-minute decision to travel four days by train down from Rhodesia, he took second. Newton had emigrated from South Africa to Rhodesia on foot, penniless and without a clear idea of what he would do next. (When he first came down to live in South Africa from his native England, he was a teacher for a while.) Never failing in resourcefulness and a love of adventure, so much at odds with his quiet manner, Newton worked for a while in the copper mines and never went back to farming. I'm not sure how he got along when his career as a professional money-earning runner came to an end, but he was never living on much more than minimal income. Still, he seemed content with what turned out to be a somewhat bohemian existence. In 1927 he ran his last Comrades for the sixth time (and fifth win) and this in spite of an early series of bad patches. At the end of the race, wrote Morris Alexander in *The Comrades Marathon Story*, Newton smoked his usual post-race cigar "with every sign of enjoyment."

In his calm and methodical way, Newton went on to set up a new world's record for 100 miles and eclipse the American Sidney Hatch's time of 16:07:43. Immediately after an ample breakfast, early on a July morning in 1927, Newton set off about his task, having never run longer than 60 miles in practice. An official car some 150 feet behind him kept the dirt road lit up with its headlamps as Newton "ambled along at a serenely easy seven miles per hour." At the halfway point there was a hotel, where a nice hot lunch, ordered in advance was set steaming upon the table. Newton sat down and polished it off in 12 minutes, consuming soup, chicken, vegetables, and a fruit pie.

The run went on into the night as Newton drank frequently from thermoses of hot tea provided by the officials. He had slowed to 6½ miles an hour trying to potter along, as he put it, "though every nerve and fiber seemed to be crying for rest." Rather uncharacteristically, Newton made it clear that he was quite exhausted at the finish, but his time of 14 hours and 43 minutes was almost 85 minutes faster than Hatch's.

The next year in Los Angeles Arthur Newton was one of 119 stalwarts drawn by the lure of a $25,000 first prize who lined up at Ascot Speedway for the start of the first of two footraces across the United States. In terms of sheer extravaganza and scope, it was the greatest organized footrace in the history of ultrarunning. The 3,422 miles of running that lay ahead included deserts and mountains as well as primitive road and camping conditions. Nothing of its kind had ever been put on before and, once again, only a fabulously energetic and self-confident promoter such as Charles C. Pyle—who was at his zenith—could have pulled it off.

3.
Across the U.S. with
Cash-and-Carry Pyle

C. C. (also known as "Cash-and-Carry") Pyle was, as eventually became apparent, not a malicious person. But his modus vivendi always seemed to necessitate living just a jump ahead of creditors and lawsuits of one kind or another. Pyle hoped that his traveling sideshow of runners and accompanying actresses, vaudeville artists and musicians would draw paying crowds at the end of each day's "stage" of running. Upon completing the marked distance, which varied between towns but was ordinarily in a range of 40 to 60 miles, each runner would retire to a tent that had been set up by the advance crew. In the evening local townspeople came into the big tent for the show.

It was not an easy experience for the runners, the vast majority of whom were undertrained for such an undertaking. Even the tough, hard core of a dozen stalwarts who ran near the front had yet to learn what such a 2-month-long grind required. Newton noticed that when football-player Red Grange fired the gun on the 4th of March 1928, a number of men took off as if they were in a 10-mile race. Newton's description of the first day or so gives an idea of some of the comforts and thorns the runners encountered. The first night began thus:

> *Yes, like the others, I turned in but that didn't mean sleep. There was a sort of circus-caravan traveling along ahead of us and performing alongside our control each night; and what with the drumming, banging, whistling and screaming which it kept up till midnight, none of us had a chance to get to sleep . . . The noise it occasioned was a very sore point with the runners throughout the trip.*
>
> *That night it started to rain, and as the tents were leaky we were not long in discovering the fact.*
>
> *Officials in cars moved up and down the line watching the contestants and providing any necessary assistance; while the Maxwell House Coffee Pot, a splendidly equipped car shaped like a great jug, took up a position twenty miles along the road to disgorge hot nourishment gratis to each runner as he came along . . .*

Within 550 miles Newton had gained a lead of 9¼ hours in total cumulative time over anyone else in the race (the idea obviously being that the winner would be the runner with the least elapsed time to complete each stage). But near Two Gun Camp, Arizona, inflamed Achilles tendons forced the Englishman out of the race, although he continued to be a part of the caravan after Pyle hired him as a "technical adviser."

With Newton's withdrawal, the lead shifted back and forth until Peter Gavuzzi, another Englishman with a very different, effervescent sort of personality but just as tenacious an approach, settled into the top spot at around 1,000 miles. Gavuzzi, who was born in England to a French mother and an Italian father, held the lead until about 3,000 miles when abscesses in his teeth made a doctor pull him out of the race.

The closing week saw some brutal 55 to 73-mile days, but 55 men finished all the same. The winner was a 20-year-old, Andy Payne of Oklahoma, a farmer's son. There were a lot of skeptical people at the time who thought that such an effort must surely be "bad" for one's health, after such an unremitting strain, but in spite of the deep fatigue felt by a number of men at the finish, a thorough check by the chief medical officer of the "Bunion Derby" left him completely satisfied that no ill effects were sustained by anyone. And the following year at Columbus Circle, some of the same competitors were back for the reverse run!

Newton and Gavuzzi, two of them, had teamed their resources and trained together near Southampton until the time came for them to book passage on the boat back to New York. Unlike the conditions for the first year's trans-U.S. race, competitors had to pay a stiff entry fee and provide their own food, lodging and handlers. On arrival in New York, Newton and Gavuzzi bought a one-ton Chevrolet van fitted with three beds (for themselves and their handler), a small refrigerator and stove, shelves, a gramophone and classical records—for which Newton had a great fondness. The comedian Will Rogers was the celebrity picked to fire the gun for the mobbed start at Columbus Circle—where, coincidentally, America's first marathon race finished in 1897 and within a quarter-mile of the finish of the present-day New York City Marathon. The competitors ran to the ferry slip on the Hudson, were levied over and sent on their way again to Elizabeth, New Jersey, and points west.

4.
Remembering the
Second Transcontinental Race

There are only a handful of survivors now from that race, for the most part old men. Peter Gavuzzi, who was again the ultimate leader in the second race, can be found in thriving retirement in the little country village of Steeple Ashton. He lives without a telephone in a simple but cozy cottage.

It was an unsettled spring day when I tramped out along the two-lane road which is flanked by open farmland and freshly plowed fields. The brief sunshine of the April afternoon gave way to a torrent of hailstones, but Gavuzzi's hearth was blazing with a coal fire. In between innumerable scratchings with a match to relight his pipe, he brewed fresh kettles of hot tea. He is a short, plump fellow, balding now, with twinkling eyes behind his glasses. He was comfortably, almost nattily attired in tie and shirt with a light pullover sweater and a warm jacket over that.

Raised a Londoner, his father was a chef who cooked at the Royal Automobile Club in London's Pall Mall. His father, Gavuzzi noted proudly, cooked for King Umberto of Italy as well. His mother was a chambermaid in the Queen's Hotel—which is how she met his father. Gavuzzi's speech, heavily Cockney, is sprinkled with "blimeys" and "cors" and "bloomin's." He's an intelligent man, thoughtful, energetic. He has clearly made his terms with life for he exudes a kind of cheerful serenity, despite the still painful memory of the way the Second Transcontinental Race ended some fifty years earlier. Perhaps he has been asked many times about the Pyle races, but he still tells his tales as if they were freshly minted.

"The Pyle race . . ." he said musingly. "It isn't the best runner who wins a race like that. It's the healthiest man who wins, the one who can keep out of trouble. I'd do a 60-mile lap, been out on the road eight or nine hours, I'd just get in, look around and the next bugger's coming in but a minute behind. But if you get a bad knee, a bad blister or something, you can lose six hours in one day. That's how easy it was, and how hard it was to lose. Now a lot of people have said some of the runners hitched rides and all

121

Peter Gavuzzi recalls the 1928 and 1929
footraces on bad roads across the U.S.

that—it's a lot of baloney. It wasn't possible. For someone to beat you as you're running along, he has to pass you. If you go along and see him in front of you, you say, hello, where did *he* come from? I'd send my trainer up to watch Johnny Salo if he was in front, to see how much of a lead he had. But Will Wiklund, his trainer, would be watching *me* to make sure I wasn't nobbin' a ride. But amongst good runners it doesn't ever come into it. The money was so important we were each watching the other.

"But round the back, cor blimey, we used to call them the sick, lame and lazy. There were about thirty of them. In the morning after the roll call, the gun would go for the start. Away we went! That pack used to turn round and go into the cafeteria and have their breakfast. Then, during the day, if they found a bridge with a river under it they'd take their stuff off and go swimming. They used to get in about five minutes before midnight, which was the deadline, singing and chatting. Sometimes they were sleeping by the side of the road during the day. It was seeing the country and getting paid a little money by their home states for doing it. The real race was in front among the first 15 or 20 men.

"The first race we didn't know anything about this kind of race. They used to frighten the life out of us in California. Wait until you get to that bloody desert, they said, it cooks you alive. Of course we didn't have the shoes you fellas have got today. We had either an ordinary leather shoe or one of those tennis shoes—plimsolls—that they go to the seaside with. The soles were made with pure crepe rubber. It wasn't the sole wearing out so much as the canvas. Take Missouri—we called it the state of misery—every day rain, rain, rain. It rotted the canvas. There was a bloke with a van who went along mending all our shoes.

"I was only 22½, very young then for a race like that. When you've got to run every day for 70-odd days, and nearly 47 miles a day average, you've got to know something about your body. It's not brawn, it's brains that wins one of them races. I thought to myself, if I do 8 miles an hour Salo's going to have to do 8½ to pass me and keep ahead. Now 8½ on a 5- or 6-hour run is going to take a lot out of him, and all he can gain is 4 or 5 minutes. That's the way I worked it, for up to 3,000 miles I had him nearly all the time. Now and again we'd come in together. I didn't gain but I didn't lose, and he never gained—it was a day lost. I had to keep doing that all the time. I could always tell whether he was running well or running dumpy. But if [Guisto] Umek, who was behind Salo in time, went forward, ah, then, Salo would wake up 'cause he couldn't let Umek pass him. Once Salo went, I had to go. That's the way it kept unfolding all the time. It was a race of who was going forward, who was going back. It was a hard thing.

"Umek was a temperamental Italian. He couldn't speak a blooming word of English so he attached himself to me because I speak the language, and he'd tell me all his troubles and blame everybody else and then in the end he used to blame me! Once in the Mojave Desert it was 105 in the shade. Umek stopped and told his trainers something. Then he went on again. They went away for nearly an hour, and when they came back they brought him a few bananas. Fancy in the desert asking for bananas. He picked them up and threw them on the ground, and walked a quarter-mile back to tell me that he had asked them for three bananas and they had only brought him two. Or we'd be running along and you'd see him underneath a tree at a table having his lunch. He was crazy, but there was no man in the world that could touch him if the distance was over 60 miles.

"Oh, I had bad times, sure. There are all these little things that this little bloke inside you tells you. I had him lots of times. Then your trainer comes along and says: 'What the bloody hell you doing? You should be running.' And you say, 'Well, you come out here and run and I'll drive the damn thing.' The thing that punished me the most was headwinds, especially being a little fellow like myself weighing 112 pounds. The main thing in a race like that is you've got to be consistent and do a good day's work every day. That's the secret of it.

"Newton was a great runner, but in the second race he got knocked over at Terre Haute, Indiana, by a car. Funny, a parson did that. His father was a parson. Newton was hoity-toity, you had to say 'Sir' to him. I must have known him over 30 years and I always addressed him as 'Sir.' He called me Pete. With educated people he was as friendly as anyone, but he wasn't so good when it came to the down-at-the-bottom business. He just didn't mix in exactly the way I mixed in with Salo and some of the others. We liked to go to the pub and have a beer and sing songs. Not him. But Newton was a nice fellow. Everybody liked him. Very clever, too. He'd come in after a lap and then he'd go in his tent and sit there and smoke in bed, and then he'd start typewriting because he used to cover the race for the London newspaper, *The News of the World*, and he used to send them an account of the entire race. That's the way he was: calm, cool, collected. He was the best-trained man in the world at that period.

"Newton used to shave every day, regular as clockwork, every whisker cut to a piece. I said to him, 'It's all very well for you, but

I'm fed up with this shaving, I'm too damn tired. When I come in I want to get a bath and eat and go to sleep.' I said 'Don't wake me up till 15 minutes before the starts.' So he said, 'Please yourself, Peter.' But by Chicago my beard was all over me so Newton said, 'Why don't you go and have it trimmed up a bit?' I fell asleep in the barber chair and when I woke up I had no beard left. And of course the papers compared it to Samson and Delilah."

Losing his beard didn't seem to sap Gavuzzi's strength. He was still holding off Johnny Salo of Passaic, New Jersey, a Finnish-American who was Gavuzzi's nearest and strongest rival throughout the 1929 race from New York to California. At the start of the last day's stage Gavuzzi had 9 minutes and 56 seconds lead on the American. The final lap began in Long Beach, California. From there the runners had four untimed miles to cover to get to Wrigley Field Stadium, where a marathon race on the field would finish the 3,665-mile race. Apparently the runners were to reassemble there and wait for the start as a group, but as the early runners came in they were waved onto the track and the race was on.

"In Los Angeles," Gavuzzi said, "one of those great big freight trains came by and took five minutes to get through, but I didn't care. If the race had counted from start to finish, it was going slow enough for me to have jumped on and then off on the other side. But when I got to the stadium the race had started. That was all unfair. I really got bunkered out of that one. The newsmen lost all their bloody bets. And at the end they said if you put down that you were cheated, you're going to be looked upon as a bad sportsman."

Johnny Salo won the day's lap with a 12-minute-and-44-second margin over his rival; he won with a cumulative elapsed time of 525 hours, 57 minutes and 20 seconds. His margin of victory was about 2 minutes and 48 seconds, certainly an eyelash considering how much time it had taken Gavuzzi and Salo to run the race. (The checks that were issued by Pyle were worthless,however, and the temporarily bankrupt promoter never paid up.) A few years later Salo died in a freak accident when he was working as a policeman at a baseball game in Passaic. A hardball struck him in the head and he died later that same day, leaving a widowed wife and two small children.

The Great Depression came in 1929 and work was hard to come by, even for professional ultrarunners. Nonetheless Newton and Gavuzzi continued their partnership and ran when they could. They had spirit and balked at little: 6-day 2-man relay races;

Will Wiklund served as handler to Johnny Salo, winner
of the 1929 race from New York to Los Angeles.

200-mile snow-shoe races from Montreal to Quebec; and on
Gavuzzi's part a number of solo runs including a 105-mile trek
carrying a letter from the mayor of Buffalo to the mayor of
Toronto. But the jobs grew scarcer and the pro indoor marathon
and ultra circuit of New York, Boston, Philadelphia, Chicago and
Los Angeles simply dried up. Newton and Gavuzzi returned home
and pursued their different careers.

During this period Newton set up a couple of remarkable feats.
In 1931, when he was almost 50 years old Newton entered a
24-hour race on a felt-and-paper 13-laps-to-the-mile indoor track
with banked sharp corners. For advice he spoke to an old-timer
who had run such a thing back in the 1880's. Others in the 7-man
field included Gavuzzi; McNamara, an Australian farmer; and
Lin Dilks of Newcastle, Pennsylvania. The temperature indoors
was about 40 degrees, and the men stopped occasionally to drink
tea or coffee, and less often to eat cheese sandwiches and fruit
salad. Used as they were to eating on the run, they plowed on,
their attention fully taken with negotiating the tight turns and
either passing or being passed by the others. Gavuzzi dropped off
with a bad leg at 20 miles. Another man, a novice at ultras,
packed it in between 60 and 70 miles. Past the 100-mile point the
runners were requested to stop for photos by the press, although
standing around because of a faulty camera cost them 9 precious
minutes. Newton shook off McNamara, who had set a new world
record for 100 miles but was now paying the price for such a hard
push early on; a cramp forced him out of the race.

As must happen sometimes in such an immense race, Newton
struggled with what seemed to be "interminable" stretches of time
and an ever-tiring body which made every mile seem "a weary
long way." He had been working his whole life to do this, he
knew, so he felt he had to hang on, no matter what:

> *I daren't look at the big clock too often—I chanced
> it about once an hour—because I was getting very tired
> myself. But I knew that if I just kept up a gentle seven
> an hour or thereabouts I'd collar the coveted record
> all right. When you get really desperately tired you
> can't keep your mind off your condition; it won't answer
> to the helm as it does when you're fighting fit, and
> I remember thinking that never again would I dream
> of risking such punishing discomfort though, hav-
> ing already undergone so much, I'd have to battle
> through the few remaining hours. Even while this*

*was passing through my mind I knew I had thought
the same thing every time I'd had a really big race,
and knew too that as soon as I had fully recovered
from the effects I should be perfectly ready to have
another and (hopefully) more successful "go" at it.*

*But I had only one job just then, and that was to
travel along with the most perfect rhythm I was
capable of; anything else and I might fail.*

Newton's professional running career came to an end in 1934
after a couple of disapointing attempts at improving on the 100-mile
record but, like Gavuzzi, he continued to be present at the various
solo and group attempts by younger men who wanted to have a
go at the London–Bath road for 100 miles, the 24-hour track runs,
and the London–Brighton road before it became an official annual
race. In fact, Newton's home in Ruislip Manor, a suburb of
London, became a regular Sunday afternoon salon of long-distance
runners. Newton never locked his door, and when he was out he
would leave a note telling whoever might have arrived to come
in, make themselves comfortable and help themselves to tea and
cake. Various South African runners who came up to train and
race were always welcome as well. Newton, who had always been
painfully shy about training in public, did his running so early in
the morning that no one ever saw him. Even as his eyesight
began to fail, and it became a source of distinct worry for his
friends that he might endanger himself, he continued to run about
100 miles a week, getting in a lifetime total of about 125,000
miles.

For the next twenty years ultrarunning was generally in a
sleepy state in England, essentially nonexistent in the States and
thriving quietly in South Africa. Some great runs did take place
but they were mostly South Africans who got involved, and not
until the disruption of World War II began to subside did the real
postwar boom in ultrarunning begin. The establishment of the
London–Brighton race in 1952 did a lot to encourage not only
English but South African and American runners as well to
train for the 52-odd-mile race. It had glamour, tradition, good
organization, tough fields, and was a lot more accessible than
distant South Africa.

5.
Notable Ultrarunners
Early and Late

It is easy—far too easy really, however understandable—to forget the existence of ultrarunners not just from a hundred but from five hundred and a thousand years ago. The records are so scanty that the deepest diver into the historical past surfaces with but half a dozen microscopic pearls. But perhaps they may serve as a chastening reminder that not all under the sun is new. If tennis sneakers and leather shoes were the lot of Edward Weston and Peter Gavuzzi, how much more must we admire the barefoot or sandal-shod Persians and Greeks who ran fabulous distances.

About 1,500 years ago one of the oldest ultraruns on record took place, according to Plutarch, when a fellow named Euchidas ran from Plataea to Delphi to fetch "sacred fire" and returned the same day, covering 113 miles in 15 hours. Such speed over rough trails stretches my credence too far, but since Plutarch was a careful historian his account was probably based on some feat in that general range. Like a lot of stories that improved with repetition, Euchidas' trip may have been speeded up a little. But Euchidas didn't just emerge out of an untrained void. Five years ago in a little periodical entitled *The Classical World*, Victor J. Mathews, a Canadian scholar, published a monograph on long-distance Greek ultrarunners, a class of men known (in the plural) as hemerodromoi, usually translated as "day runners." They were specially trained couriers who did service for cities or armies. The most famous hemerodromos was Pheidippides who, in addition to possibly having run from Marathon to Athens, had done something much more remarkable a few days earlier. He ran from Athens to Sparta on a mission, a distance of some 136 miles, in about 44 hours. Appropriately the patron god of the hemerodromoi was Hermes, himself a fleet-footed messenger.

According to Mathews, communications in Asia Minor under the Persian Empire depended as well on couriers who ran long distances. Among a few other tidbits he lets fall, one of the most startling is Pliny's account of an 8-year-old boy who ran around the Circus Maximus apparently doing about 68 miles in 9 hours, a respectable time for a man three times that age.

Ultrarelays such as that run by the team of Los Angeles policemen from L.A. to Montreal, a distance of almost 4,000 miles in 21 days, in 1976, are descendants of an honorable tradition. Most ultrarunning in antiquity was encouraged for practical reasons, not for sport or personal challenge. *The Handbook of South American Indians* gives the following account of Inca messengers:

> *The Inca maintained a postal service along the main roads to relay messages back and forth to the capital. Every ¼ or ½ league along the main roads was a pair of huts, one on each side of the road, each hut sheltering two runners (caski). ... One Indian from each hut was always on the watch for messages, presumably watching in opposite directions. When a messenger arrived, the waiting runner ran beside him to receive the drop, usually a short verbal message perhaps accompanied by a quipu or other object, and carried it to the next post. In this way, a very high average speed could be kept up. ... The men were trained from boyhood, and were subject to very severe punishments for failure to deliver messages.*
>
> *The average speed of the runners was about 50 leagues a day (probably 150 miles or 240 kilometers). ... The Emperor had fresh fish brought to him from the Coast in two days.*

I might add that no trace of professional running remains anymore in the Inca Empire that once extended beyond Peru up into Ecuador. While I ran on the roads in the outback of those countries, whole families would empty out of their homes to watch silently as I padded past, a remarkable novelty for people who no longer carry on the ultrarunning traditions of their forebears.

The same rigorous style of living undoubtedly fostered other Indian ultrarunners in Central and North America. From the Museum of Natural History in New York, I derived the following bits of information.

- Among the Chitimacha tribe of Mississippi, some adult runners trained "so assiduously that wonderful stories were told of their swiftness." It was said of "one of them that he could defeat a horse within a space of a five- or six-acre lot."
- Among the Papago of Arizona and Sonora, Mexico, were

2-man kickball races over 20 miles in length. Once when making a trip to get medicine power, two young men left for a distant salt bed at midnight and returned the next morning, 10 hours later, having run almost continuously.

Among the Fox Indians in eastern Wisconsin were so-called ceremonial runners, who purified themselves with 10-day fasts, drank only water on their runs and wore buffalo-hide moccassins. One report mentions rather vaguely that a ceremonial runner went from Green Bay to the edge of the Missouri River, where the Sauks were living, to warn them of impending trouble with other Indian tribes. After resting four days the runner returned. It might well have been a trip each way of 400 miles.

Ceremonial runners have also been reported among other North American Indian groups, including the Creek, Kansa, Omaha and Osage. Unfortunately, details about their runs are exceedingly scanty and rarely firsthand. A few reports provide just a little more information. About the Opate tribe of Mexico described by John Bartlett, an American anthropologist in the nineteenth century, as very brave fighters, we also learn that: "They are excellent couriers, and are often employed to carry messages long distances on foot, running the greater portion on the way. In twenty-four hours, they have been known to run from 40–50 leagues (about 120–150 miles)." And Robert H. Lowie has this to say about the Plateau Shoshoneans of Nevada, Utah and Colorado: "A strong man might also run down an antelope by tracking it for one or two days before shooting at all."

I hardly mean to suggest a bias against the continents of Asia, Africa and greater Europe, for I did find a few scattered citations of early ultrarunning feats there, particularly when it came to tracking, or trailing game for long periods of time. Probably the need for such ultra abilities stretches, among certain groups, way back into what will remain forever the uncharted vastness of man's prehistory, when written records simply were not made and the pressure to survive as a hunting-gathering group meant an all-day commitment to looking for food. Twelve years ago, in an issue of a now defunct British athletic monthly, *Athletics Arena*, one author mentioned "half-a-dozen pastoral tribes with ability that may one day set the World aflame." He mentioned particularly the Masai of Kenya, who pursue game to exhaustion, and the Karamojong of Uganda. The Karamojong reputedly cover 40 miles at a whack while tending cattle, stealing cattle or making war.

Two Mexican tribes remarkable for their ultra fleetness and toughness among native groups around the world are the Seri Indians and the Tarahumara, both found in northern Mexico. The Seri Indians, a small and still extremely timid group, live on the Island of Tiburón in the Gulf of California. Deserts and mountainous terrain on either side of the mainland have throughout their history enforced minimal contact with other peoples, including native Mexicans. Tiburón itself is a hot and extremely barren place with rough, hilly trails crisscrossing the island. A 1945 report described the natives as "a homeless burden-bearing people, wandering in family groups or clans. The distance between reliable food sources in the sea and supplies of fresh water created a pedestrian habit whereby they acquired a remarkable fleetness of foot." The name itself means "the speed of one who runs."

An 80-year-old report on the Seris mentions in passing a Seri mother who was desperately anxious about the welfare of her sick 12-month-old baby. At nightfall she set off with her child, hoping to get medicine from a white person. By "dawn next morning she was at Molino del Encinas, 17 leagues (nearly 45 miles) away, with her helpless child and a peace offering in the form of a hare, which she had run down and caught in the course of the journey."

So poverty stricken are the Seri Indians that their diet has included the pitahaya, a cactus fruit whose pulp is about the size of a plum. After the seeds are excreted from the body in the feces, they grind them up with water or mix them with green sea-turtle paste and reconsume them. It is hardly fair, however, to imagine them as a grimace-faced lot, shuffling along interminably. Not only are they renowned for their speed but their grace:

> *To one familiar with the strikingly light movement characteristic of the Seri—a movement far lighter than that of the professional springer or of the thoroughbred "collected" by a skillful equestrian ... it is the habit of the errant Seri to roam spryly and swiftly on soundless tiptoes, to come and go like fleeting shadows of passing cloudlets, and on detection to slip behind shrub or rock, and into the distance so lightly as to make no audible sign or visible trail, yet so fleetly withal as to evade the hard-riding horseman.*

Yet far more remarkable than the Seri, according to what is known of them so far, are the Tarahumara Indians, who live in the pine-covered canyons and plateaus of the Sierra Madre in northern Mexico. These Indian runners not only use their ultra skills to track game and to carry messages and supplies, they develop their long-distance running ability in contests where they sometimes go 150 miles or more without stopping. Races last up to 48 hours reputedly without rest. Their average speed is not great but considering the terrain, the rough sandals they wear and their own scanty diet, I think the Tarahumara are an impressive, really remarkable group of people.

In 1975, driven by an unquenchable curiosity and the vague hope that I might learn something about running from them, I set off for their homeland in the state of Chihuahua, which borders on the state of Texas. It was part of a trip overland I was making from El Paso to the Amazon River, and my time was very short—a disadvantage when dropping in for lightning visits with Indian groups whose language and culture are profoundly different from my own. I soon realized that to develop a good feeling for the details of their running and their ongoing lives would have meant a long stay. The Tarahumara are renowned for their profound timidity, not only with strangers but to some degree with each other. They are not unfriendly but they are sensitive, stoic and stolid. They are comfortable during long stretches of solitude, herding sheep or sitting in the sun on a rock, a blanket wrapped around them, just looking about.

From the early 1600's right through to today, the Tarahumara have stubbornly spurned the approaches of both Mexican settlers and priests. The former sought lumber, land, gold and silver, as well as cheap Indian labor. The latter were after souls, and to avoid both groups the Tarahumara either fought back or retreated. They now live in the upper section of the Urique River. Although a north-south train line passes through part of Tarahumaraland, it is (in spite of its forested beauty) a difficult, underdeveloped area that strongly resists the casual intruder. An occasional gringo will come down from the border to go backpacking in the famous Copper Canyon, but any serious attempt at penetrating this region meets several problems. There are no roads; at best, rough foot trails dip along down the steep sides of the gorges that cut through the region. There are a few mission settlements linked by an airplane owned by the local priests, and there are mules for hire for iron-bottomed travelers.

Although the Tarahumara have been affected by goods available from the outside world, basically their lives are not too different from the way they were a thousand years ago. Daily life is restricted to crude farming of corn, potatoes and beans and to a little sheepherding and cattle raising. Their average caloric intake has been estimated at 1,500 daily, which contrasts with the average American daily food intake of 3,000. For the most part they are fairly short; their skin is a beautiful dark copper color; they have black hair and thin, wiry legs. For them hard labor is not just a way of life; it is a necessity. It is, so to speak, the training for their running, though they do not think of it that way.

Here are some of their characteristics, recorded by various observers in the last century and this:

- They carry wood on their backs with a carrying strap, piling up 3-to 4-foot-long logs to make a load "that would stagger a burro."
- They carry crates of fruit on their back to market towns, the round trip sometimes taking up to 5 days.
- They are frequently known to run 170 miles without stopping.
- "A man has been known to carry a letter in 5 days from Guazapares to Chihuahua and back, a distance of nearly 600 miles."
- They were once frequently hired to run wild horses into the corral, requiring 2 to 3 days.
- They run down deer, "following it for days through snow and rain . . . until it is overtaken utterly jaded and its hoofs dropping off."

The focus of their play is on running games, in which men, women and children participate but in their own variations. Commonly, interest in preparing for a race begins when one set of runners challenges another team. The Tarahumara live in caves and houses separated from their neighbors, but although they have no towns they do identify themselves with a certain "pueblo" or locale. Talk becomes excited and the betting is avid, all the more so perhaps since blankets, sheep, food and items of clothing are so precious in such a poor society. As race day approaches the shamans, or healers, of each team employ their best magic and advice to ready the runners for the coming trial.

The common ball cactus is a "strong" plant, so runners daub themselves with the chewed roots for the three days preceding the race. "They carry the roots in their belt to make them lighter on foot and to ward off evil magic. The runners are said to fear neither fire, water, nor the dreaded smoke of the *kotcínowa* if they have the roots with them. During a race, the shaman continually chews a bit to have it ready for the runners who tire."

Frank Bozanich on his way to a new American
record for 100 kilometers, Miami, 1979.

The shamans frequently try to employ black magic, say, by digging up a right tibia from a burial cave and offering food, beer and a cross as tribute to the dead so that the opponents will be weakened. Or he may bury a bone in a spot where the other team will be running. For the same reason the smoke of a potent little cigar, composed of the dried blood of a bat and a turtle mixed together with tobacco, may be blown onto the rival runners.

Each team sets off from a marked point, usually on a loop course of some length, kicking along a small wooden ball carved from the root of an oak tree. The lead runner will kick it along, follow to where it lands, kick again and so continue. Hands cannot be used to propel the ball forward. "The racers wear rattles of deer-hoofs and bits of reeds tied together on a strip of leather. . . . The magic rattling keeps them from falling asleep while running, so they say; besides, the deer-hoofs lend them the swiftness of the stag." The average speed is about 6 to 6½ miles an hour. .

It may be of interest to compare ultra- and marathon runners in Europe and the U.S. and South Africa, whose own pre-race fetishes may center on diet as irrationally as the Tarahumara. It is easy to read these notes on the Indians with a slightly condescending smile, but most runners have favorite caps, shirts, ways of cutting their hair, set rituals before a big race—the objective value of such things, I think, hardly matters if it adds to the power one believes one accumulates thereby. Surely belief in self or belief in something will animate and sustain the body to a degree far beyond ordinary bounds. In any case, the old athletic bugaboo about forbidding sex before a race applies to the Tarahumara. But of special interest is the prohibition against "fat, potatoes, eggs, and anything sweet . . . but rabbits, deer, rats, turkeys, and chaparral-cocks are wholesome, and such nourishment enables them to win."

The "carbohydrate-loading diet," which is repeated as frequently as a religious litany in the pages of running magazines, is a diet whereby a runner depletes the body's glycogen stores in the muscles by eating primarily protein. Then a switch is made to carbohydrate-rich foods, creating a temporary overload of glycogen and, in theory, a store of energy that will put off the inevitable slowdown in a long race. Since a high percentage of the body's fuel in a race depends on fat burning in addition to glycogen—and the more so the longer the race, are the Tarahumara so deluded or not? One research physiologist in New York, Dr. Edward Colt, has speculated rather critically on the presumed effectiveness of the carbo-loading diet for well-trained runners. Its helpfulness may simply be marginal for them, he feels. And yet there are runners who swear by it. Such disruptive and unsettling evidence makes me feel a bit of sardonic amusement and relief—all the answers are not yet in and perhaps there is time to continue to admire the inspired guesswork and childish beliefs that sustain ultra bulldogs.

The Tarahumara women have their own kind of race, again between teams, but using a grapevine hoop which they fling with a forked stick. Although their races are shorter, they may go on all night as well and spectators light the track with flaming torches. Naturally the children imitate their elders and can sometimes be seen scampering along as fully intense and excited as the adults. There have been a few attempts to bring the Tarahumara runners into international competition, one notable example taking place in 1929 in Los Angeles, when Paavo Nurmi ran against several Tarahumara men and women—and won. (The Indians stopped when they heard the bell signaling the start of the last lap, thinking for a moment that the race was over.) As with the Bushmen of the Kalahari desert of South Africa, who are also renowned for their great ultrarunning when they pursue game with a minimum of water intake for themselves, there are problems of motivation. Taken out of their own culture, the Tarahumara have not seemed to respond with much enthusiasm to our way of doing things. One South African runner who visited the Bushmen told me that it was hard for them, as they did not have races even as the Tarahumara do, to want to run for hours in a circle around a track.

It is important not to forget, too, that the Tarahumara are not so very different from us, either. It can get quite cold in the winter at 6,000 feet, even in Mexico, and I remember asking my young Tarahumara guide who spoke Spanish if the Tarahumara felt the cold or if they grew accustomed to it. He was halfway Mexicanized himself, but he still wore a bright white headband in spite of his boots and jeans and zip-up jacket. "Oh, no," he said, turning to look at me as we walked along the trail. "They feel the cold very much. They simply have to put up with it."

It was a windy day on the plateau, and patches of ice were still tucked in among the outbreaks of rock. We stopped at the house of his grandfather, an elder of the pueblo and an official called a *gobernador*, a fine old man with a lined face who could not be rushed. We sat for a long time slowly working our way around to questioning him about the possibility of seeing a footrace. In the distance dogs barked and the bells of the sheep tinkled. Some small boys stared with that deep shyness of country people and said not a word. After the slow parleying, the upshot was that the local Indians had gotten drunk on tesguino, a kind of corn brew, since it was just after the all-night New Year's mass. I was disappointed, but we pushed on through the pine forests and the silent fields taking a long way back to the mission.

The sounds of a violin floated out into the afternoon, and in a small clearing we saw Indians lying in the sun drinking tesguino. Far from being the stolid sorts I had met before who sat up all night wrapped in their blankets, sucking silently on their hand-rolleds, they were a lively group and we were invited into the darkness of the little house, which was ripe with the usual Indian smell of unwashed bodies. There was a good deal of discussion about my running shoes. The women, who sat on the ground, with their bare feet and babies slung in shawls on their backs, listened and giggled among themselves. There was a simplicity and ridiculousness about some of the antics that corn mash inspired in all of us, and it was with some difficulty that we at last extricated ourselves for the long hike back.

In a way I hope that the Tarahumara are left to practice their ultrarunning games among themselves, on their own terms. Although I never did see them race, Conrad Lemholtz's description in the early 1900's of the race at nightfall continues to linger in my mind as a final impression: "As darkness comes on, torches of resinous pine wood are lighted and carried along to illuminate the path for the runners, that they may not stumble, making the scene one of extreme picturesqueness, as those torchbearers, demon-like, hurry through the forest."

From the remote mountain areas of Tibet came a report first published some fifty years ago about a class of ultrarunners so unusual, so swift and so able to endure immense trips that it strains credulity. It is difficult to know how much one can rely on the accounts provided by the author, Alexandra David-Neel. David-Neel was born in Paris and ever since she was a child yearned to travel in Tibet, which she eventually did as a lone pilgrim. Her major interest was in a serious study of Tibetan Buddhism involving complex and often fantastical-sounding practices, which she detailed in *Magic and Mystery in Tibet*, first published in the early 1930's.

Traveling in northern Tibet she got her first rare glimpse of a *lung-gom-pa* runner. The phrase *lung-gom* refers to a branch of special training which develops both mental concentration and physical adeptness of various kinds. *Lung-gom* "is said to develop uncommon nimbleness and especially enables its adepts to take extraordinary long tramps with amazing rapidity." These ultra-runners apparently could cover a period of several days without sleep. As it was, Madame David-Neel was immensely curious and stopped the figure who approached her party across the grassy tableland to find out more about his training. She was warned that being spoken to would "break" the man's meditative state and kill him. Dubious as she was about such a dramatic result, Madame David-Neel felt nonetheless that his nerves would be painfully shocked if disturbed in his trancelike state and decided she couldn't offend local customs, given her hard-won acceptance by the lamas as a rare foreigner. However, she noted the *lung-gom-pa*'s dress and gait.

> *I could clearly see his perfectly calm, impassive face and wide-open eyes, with their gaze fixed on some invisible far-distant object situated somewhere high up in space. The man did not run. He seemed to lift himself from the ground, proceeding by leaps. It looked as if he had been endowed with the elasticity of a ball and rebounded each time his feet touched the ground. His steps had the regularity of a pendulum. He wore the usual monastic robe and toga, both rather ragged. His left hand gripped a fold of the toga and was half hidden under the cloth. The right held a phurba (magic dagger).*

By quizzing herdsmen she met a little later on her trip, Madame David-Neel calculated that he must have traveled at that speed for 24 hours without stopping.

An old legend explains that these runners were periodically called upon to gather demons from various parts in order to appease Shinjed, the Lord of Death. If the story was true, training for *lung-gom-pas* was first developed in the 1300's. Developing *lung-gom* skill required work on breathing exercises and the recitation of a mantra, silently recited in rhythm with footsteps and breathing. "The walker must neither speak, nor look from side to side. He must keep his eyes fixed on a single distant object and never allow his attention to be attracted by anything else. . . . Though normal consciousness is for the greater part suppressed, it remains sufficiently alive to keep the man aware of the obstacles in his way, and mindful of his direction and goal."

It is a description that might well apply to any great ultrarunner in deep concentration on the work.

Michael Koenig, a 2:28 marathoner, tries his hand at an ultra.

4.
SOLO ARTISTS, CRAZIES AND GREAT ACHIEVERS

1.
A Tiny Democracy
of Determined Spirits

Around the world, ultrarunning attracts a tiny democracy of citizens whose numbers include not just the fleet of foot but the so-called "backmarkers," and not just men but even a few women. In this group there is ample room for the crazies, the solo artists and the great achievers to express themselves.

In street clothes these runners, these monsters of achievement, are nothing special to behold. Without a paper number pinned to their chest to stimulate them into fiery concentration, they seem good-humored and even capable of praising their rivals with a fair degree of generosity. The odor of armpits and Ben Gay, the sound of a pursed mouth ejecting spittle, an angry voice demanding this or that from a harried camp-follower—those frailer, earthy moments are not often apparent. I have to surmise from slight intonations the determination that must always lie underneath. If they are shy and silent, I assume that merely cloaks the raging will underneath, and if they are hearty types happiest wrapping their hands around a stein of ale, then I deduce that their confidence is all on the surface! But I know, with a bit more penetration than that, that not a one of them is just a boring automaton constructing paper goals.

It isn't easy to pick one's way through the immense briar patch that lies between oneself and the ever-receding phantom of achievement and rest. Well, never rest. (That last word puts me in mind of Wally Hayward, whose massive but controlled impatience still drives him out along the roads of Johannesburg at the age of 71 for 50-mile training runs.) And it is not just the prime fanatics themselves who write the recipe for success. It is the wives, the husbands, the girlfriends, the parents, the close friends and the strangers alike who, for the most part, perform unstintingly to make these runs a success. On the sidelines of races around the world I've witnessed not only the efforts of the runners but also those of their supporters.

Morris Alexander, a South African journalist, dedicated his book, *The Comrades Marathon Story*, "to all marathon widows and in particular to my late wife Nesta, who was my marathon widow." The grand obsession required if one hopes to do well, which is on the infantile scale of self-absorption, is not easy without someone cooking meals and changing diapers. Bernard Gomersall, one of the great English ultrarunners in the 1960's, mentions with quiet emotion how for 12 years he and his wife, Ruth, went out once a year socially. Everything else was subsumed to the running. "Ruth had to suffer," he said, "so it's been great at last to put running fifth or sixth in our lives and go out and do other things." There is no regret on either side for the achievement they forged together, but neither denies that there was a cost.

And there are others who help it to happen. You also do it because of those other runners who came before you and set a standard. Because of the presence of other runners, you pull out of yourself speeds you could never sustain on your own. You need enthusiastic officials to hold watches in the rain and scribble on bits of paper. You need handlers. You need a point-to-point run across a piece of country that no one else has gotten to yet—a sort of negative help! And there isn't a soul out there who doesn't enjoy a little encouragement and praise, even if it's on a tiny scale. Because at most of these races, the spectator crowds wouldn't come close to filling a New York City subway platform.

One misconception I should like to lay to rest is the myth of the "strong and silent" long-distance runner. They may pretend to have talked themselves out on the subject, thank you, but once launched these runners are happy to go on talking indefinitely. Carol Gomersall likes to say that when an ultra man stops talking, it's time to bury him. Recalling her frequent attendance at ultraraces all over England with an only child, Bernadette, she said: "I think I've spent most of my time sitting on walls outside schools, churches and all sorts of very uninteresting places waiting while Bernard got changed. He was always the last one out. We used to just sit there and wait—blowing with gale, pouring with rain—waiting for him to stop talking to his friends and come along."

Ultramarathoning offers a variety of options for different temperaments, tastes and budgets. Some runners will try anything as long as it's running, but others abhor the notion of 200 turns around a cinder oval. Used to the roads, they need to feel they are running *to* somewhere. Those with incurable wanderlust go off on runs that might last months, where the pressure to run a large section of every day, even if not at full effort, is a very different task from running a blow-out hard race just once.

There are a number of feats and attempts at various kinds of records that I have simply not been able to track down in any detail. Many of them could probably merit a book on their own. There is, for example, the dubious category of "non-stop" running records. New Zealander Max Telford has current possession of the record, which he got by running 186 miles (300 kilometers) in 31:33:38 at Waialua. The "rules" allow no more than 5 minutes per hour for toilet, changing shoes or medical attention. Purists find nonstop running a little questionable. What if a runner needs 10 minutes in one hour and skips a stop the next? Will he be disqualified, and who is there to watch, et cetera? Probably the "purest" non-stop run was American Jared Bead's 1969 run of 122 miles without a single stop.

Telford has run across—or more precisely, down and up—the Grand Canyon and back again. In 1976 he ran across Death Valley, covering 120 miles in 19 hours and 17 minutes. That was in January. In July he repeated the effort and then, in a dazzling bit of lunacy, ran back across again. This time it took him 73 hours to complete the 240 miles. When he finished he wept. When his wife said she had never before seen him cry after an ultra effort, he answered tersely that he had never been in hell before.

Telford's list of accomplishments goes on and on, but one of his most recent long runs was a 1977 trans-Canada run of 5,198 miles in 106 days! In an interview about the Canadian run, Telford commented later: "I was in fantastic physical shape when I finished, but psychologically I was shattered. I was really shattered, you know. It's just the same as that first marathon you run. You know your body can run it, but it's the mind that drives it along."

Then there is the Lakeland 24-hour run, which is the special preserve of fell runners. "Fells" refer to the extremely hilly terrain of the Lake District in England, where sheepherders and country types who are used to the rough terrain and rocky footpaths scamper up and down like mountain goats. Most fell races are anywhere from several to 10 miles in length. In the Lakeland 24-Hour, the idea is to cross all of the summits the previous record holder has reached and then squeeze in as many more as possible. Joss Naylor, a sheepherder with a bad back that periodically lays him low, set the current record in 1975 when he covered 72 peaks, ascending and descending about 40,000 feet in the process. The linear distance was 105 miles.

There are any number of journey runs which I will only mention in passing. The Pennine Way run follows the course of a national walking trail in England that is 271½ miles long. A good deal of the course is over 1,200 feet in altitude, but it sometimes goes much higher, as at Cheviot (2,676 feet), Cross Fell (2,930 feet) and Pen-Y-Ghent (2,274 feet). According to Andy Milroy, temperature and wind force at 2,000 feet in Britain are equivalent to about 8,000 feet in the Continental Alps. In 1974, Joss Naylor covered the course in 3 days, 4 hours and 36 minutes, but the present speed champion over this greatly varying terrain is Peter Dawes, who did it 2 hours and 48 minutes faster. Dawes ran 90½ miles the first day, 96 miles the second and 84 miles the third.

Another favorite for the English has been the 876-mile Land's End to John O'Groats Run, which goes from one end of England to another. It has often been run as a relay effort and, needless to say, it's been walked various times. In 1977 it took Fred Hicks 10 days and 3½ hours of elapsed time to scuttle the length of the United Kingdom, although the actual running time was 154 hours and 15 minutes, almost 15½ hours of running a day! In spite of incessant headwinds, he usually covered between 77 and 91 miles daily, averaging between 10 and 11 minutes per mile. Hicks reported later that his appetite was off for a day or two but soon increased tremendously. He was particularly fond of orange squash (a sweetened juice concentrate), sweet tea, homemade fruit cake, cheese and health food nutrition bars. His gastronomic excesses apparently nearly kept pace with his physical ones, for he had lost only two pounds when he finished.

A New Zealander particularly worthy of mention is Siegfried Bauer, whose short frame and tousled head of hair crop up every once in a while in photos of some madcap running business. In 1975 Bauer ran the length of New Zealand from the Bluff to Cape Reinga, 1,335 miles, in 18 days, 5 hours and 1 minute, an average of 70 miles a day. He also won a 1,000-mile race from Pretoria to Capetown in 13 days and 23 hours. In 1978 he ran 1,169 kilometers, the length of Germany, in 8 days, 12 hours and 12 minutes, averaging a stupendous 85 miles a day, and getting by on less than 5 hours of sleep a night.

2.
The Twenty-Four Hour Runs

"Twenty-four hours" has a fine, primitive quality to it. In common with the Stonehenge peoples or the Sumerians or the Incas, the full cycle of a day—as the sun rises, falls and rises again—has an obvious unity that satisfies the imagination of ultra enthusiasts. For them, it has the added benefit of a special, if very simple violation of the ordinary pattern of living—there is no chance to sleep. There *are* runs now being staged of an even more extreme duration. In 1979, Don Choi organized two 48-hour runs in California. Mutterings are occasionally heard from Tom Osler in New Jersey about possibly restaging a 6-day wobble. But these feverish outbreaks are minimal, and for the most part the 24-hour run is the longest standardized track ultra now found around the world. They date back to the 6-day wobbles, when intermediate records for 100 miles and 24 hours were set up on the way to the completion of the entire 144-hour trek.

Don Turner, president of the English RRC, is a bluff, stocky, fellow, good natured in the extreme, who has a longish history of running ultras as a competitor and setting them up as an organizer. At a pub in central London, during a lunch-hour break from his job as a government auditor, he ticked off each of the individuals needed to stage a successful 24-hour run. They include a starter, an honorary referee, the 3 judges who serve as the referee's henchmen, a chief timekeeper and 8 additional timekeepers (5 at any one time should be there), 50 lap recorders (20 at any one time should be there, one each for up to 20 competitors,), 3 people in the press box to make occasional announcements, handlers for the competitors, and several persons to get sandwiches and tea for the officials.

"It's quite incredible when the starter fires a gun with 5 minutes to go and everyone starts sprinting after 23 hours and 55 minutes of slogging around! Then at the final gun, a peg goes in the track to measure where you were at the last instant."

Following Newton's great record-breaking effort in 1931, the next successful try for a longer distance came about twenty-two years later when Wally Hayward, a building inspector in Johannesburg, South Africa, traveled to England for another purpose altogether—a new London–Brighton record, if possible. Like his predecessor, Hayward was not a young man by usual athletic standards, but he was hardly the sort to be daunted by ordinary limitations and he set about his work in a methodical and rigorous fashion. He was 45 years old when he took the boat up to England, and already had years of track running and marathoning behind him; not only had he represented South Africa in the 6-mile at the Empire Games in Sydney in 1938, he also ran the marathon in the Helsinki Olympics of 1952. The two countrymen who joined him in England in 1953—Jackie Mekler and Fred Morrison—are both still very much alive and thriving, although they have retired from active competition. They shake their heads about Wally—"Wonderful Wally," as he has been dubbed by the South African press, in wonderment over the man's stubbornness and determination.

Hayward and Morrison are the best of pals, although their friendship can be punctuated by amiably pigheaded disagreement. The two of them scooped me up one evening off the steps of City Hall in downtown Johannesburg and bore me off to a Chinese restaurant for an evening of ultra talk. As Morrison piloted the small yellow car, there was a series of disagreements about navigation which were never resolved, causing our craft to rattle about through a maze of dead-end turns, unexpected exit ramps and other assorted hazards of the motorway. We did finally arrive at our destination and in between orders of wonton soup and Moo Shu pork, talk soon centered on the 24-hour run at Motspur Park in 1953. The two men are a study in counterpoint. Morrison is tallish, with wavy white hair and the smooth manner of the bon vivant and raconteur. He delights in the drama of personalities and races, but only one runner can ever rank at the top (for his fiery-tempered soul) and that is his beloved Wally.

"The man is bloody incredible," he says, talking about Hayward as a guide might speak of the immense portals of a nearby cathedral. It was as if Wonderful Wally himself were not sitting there quietly beside him. "Have you seen his calves?" Morrison asked earnestly. "Bloody incredible!" I thought for an instant that Morrison might reach over and pull up Hayward's pants legs to prove his point. They are remarkable legs, with calf muscles as solid and chunky as great table legs hewn from oak. I knew so from the photos. Runner John Dixon had given me one photo earlier in England which I had studied carefully. It showed Hayward running on the cinder track at Motspur Park, wearing white running shoes and reaching across his chest with his right hand to

In his day Wally Hayward was one of
the world's best ultra runners.

get a drink from a beaming Arthur Newton, who was standing by the side dressed in tie and jacket underneath a tremendous dark greatcoat to protect him from the chill. His hair was silvery then and brushed back carefully, and the scrub mustache was white as well. His left hand could be seen dangling out of the sleeve of his overcoat, thumb pinched between second and third fingers in a tight fist. There was something a little unusual about that gesture, as if the man's deep social shyness revealed itself in that tense little bit. Like white-skinned peas in a pod, the other runners show up coming around the curve, one after another at that point, 20-or 30-odd miles into the run. Soon enough they got scattered by the violent winds one encounters on such an effort, although lanky Derek Reynolds ran one of the less appreciated attempts of the post-Second World War era. He just happened to be second, covering 154 miles, 1,226 yards.

Hayward, of course, went on to justify everyone's confidence. He had broken the London–Brighton record by over 20 minutes and annexed Ballington's Bath–London 100-mile record. It was Newton who suggested the 24-hour track run as a final "hat trick." A stiff bout of training was aided by Newton.

"You know, Newton used to go out on every one of Mekler and Hayward's runs," Morrison said. "I was having a bit of trouble and I couldn't. He would have thermos flasks of hot water and tea and cake on his push bike. The runs were up to 50 miles in length and he was a man well over 70! He was blind as a bat. It was just after the war and we took a 400-pound box of food with us."

Although Mekler and Morrison had to return to South Africa before the 24-hour race, Newton and Peter Gavuzzi, like two fond ultra uncles, helped Hayward figure out a schedule for the race. During the run Hayward ate egg custard and rice and drank warm lemon juice "laced with sugar and salt," as well as sweetened tea and coffee. In all, the South African consumed two pounds of sugar in 24 hours—all of it in solution in the various drinks. Hayward looked at me at one point in the meal and said, to my surprise: "I made a hash of it." He had, it turned out, expected to go considerably further than he did.

"Peter Gavuzzi said to me after you do a hundred miles, come off and we'll give you a good rubdown. It'll clear the mental side up. But it was the biggest mistake I made. Rigor mortis set in and I couldn't get going again."

Morrison interrupted: "Both Newton and Gavuzzi had this theory that you had to put in a lot of miles early so as to make up for the bad spell later on. But one should never change one's speed. We had worked out that Wally was going to do about 170-odd miles in that 24 hours. When I heard that he had done 90 miles so fast, why then I knew he could never have sustained it." (At 90 miles Hayward was clocked in 11:21:51.)

Hayward's dark eyes were set deep in his face and he spoke with a very simple firmness. I could imagine him on the track, never smiling, raising his hand occasionally to signal what kind of drink he wanted so he wouldn't have to waste a syllable. What he said next was not only not a surprise but seemed a reasonable statement from someone so thoroughly immoderate in his goals.

"But look, I want to give it a go again if all goes well. I don't say I'm going to break the 150-mile mark, but I just want to see what I can do at my age."

At the 1953 24-hour run, Hayward could hardly continue after a shower and a massage at the 100-mile point, which he passed through in just over 12¾ hours. A half hour later, with some persuasion from his handlers, he got back on the track and walked and ran until—according to one description—he settled into a relatively heavy and awkward style. The 7- to 8-minutes-per-mile running of the early stages of the race had sunk to about 11 minutes per mile by the finish. One of the other runners was so stricken with fatigue that he occasionally ran into the fence. Hayward himself was handed some scalding hot tea in a paper cup. He sipped it, complained that it was cold and threw it away—a symptom of deep fatigue. He had lost 7 pounds by the end of the race. His final mileage: 159 miles, 562 yards. He said it had been a terrible race, a very hard one, and that if anyone broke his record, good luck to them.

Such luck did not come to anyone until 20 years later. In 1973, at a track in Walton-on-Thames, Ron Bentley, an Englishman, ran 161 miles, 545 yards—still the current official record. Bentley was a runner for the Tipton Harriers, a running club in the Birmingham area of England, a rough-and-tumble working-class section of England. "Ah, those Tipton boys," people told me and smiled, conjuring up notions of hard-bitten, bluff, tough-minded, high-spirited fellows. The Tipton Club was once an unbeatable bunch of blokes who stormed through ultraraces to carry off the silver booty of first-place team. In recent years, however, they have been eclipsed by other running clubs, such as the South London Harriers in the competition for the keenly contested team prizes which are more highly valued in England than in the States.

It was a hot spring day as I walked along through the suburban area where Bentley now lives, a street of pleasant homes with roly-poly hills stretching away to the horizon littered with small brick apartment dwellings. Not far away are the stacks and power lines and rail crossings of an industrial center. In the garage of a new home he was building I found Ron Bentley, immediately recognizable with his ginger mustache cut handlebar style. There was a circular bald patch on the back of his wavy head of hair. The veins stood out on his powerful forearms as he stood by a whirring electric concrete mixer wearing a red T-shirt, work pants and rubber boots. He was short and when he glanced up he greeted me genially, a little quiet in his manner until he warmed up, as he did easily enough.

We parked ourselves in the unfinished litter of the living room and soon the immense self-assurance of the man made itself clear. His rapid-fire Midlands accent was pockmarked with bursts of laughter. Clearly the 24-hour run was one of the greatest things he ever did—if one can presume to guess at such things, Certainly he had seen his goal and grasped it, and nothing will ever diminish his pleasure in such a clean effort. In a milder way than Hayward, it was clear that he wished he had tucked the cookie box a few shelves higher so the next man up would not find it quite so easy to pluck down.

Seconds after he finished in 1973, he told a reporter for *Athletics Weekly*: "I feel absolutely marvelous. I can sit back and enjoy fame. I've trained all my life for it and I've got it. I've broken the world record. I always thought I would break the record. I felt very confident. I never felt like giving up and when I was close to it I kept on pushing. I kept to a schedule. When I got tired, I eased and I had something to eat and then got back to it again. I knew once I got past the hundred miles I had done it. I had a few bad patches afterward but I recovered fairly well."

From elsewhere in the house came the excitement of the Wembley Cup Final on television, the season's-end soccer match. The low howling of the crowds sounded like wolves. Bentley's wife brought in tea and coffee as her husband explained how he, like so many other English runners, had been with the Tipton Harriers since he was a kid—28 years in fact. He now works for them as one of their team managers, and thus continues to put himself back into the sport when he has some free time from his job as one of the directors in a steel company.

He was always running "as a lad, but I never could see me as a runner." His advance into the ultras took time. Early on he ran one race with the flu and developed an inflammation of the

Ron Bentley of Tipton Harriers, England, has run 161
miles 545 yards in 24 hours, the official world's record.

heart—it took him three years to recover. He ran his marathon in 1957, finished third with a 2.49 time, certainly a quite respectable showing but vowed never to do it again because he felt so sick at the end. In 1964 he ran the London–Brighton race for the first time to help out some teammates, and at the end of *that* race he swore never to run so long again. He has since run it 10 more times. He set up for himself in business. Once his firm was well established, he devoted his energies to more serious training and such exploits as winning the Exeter–Plymouth 44-miler with a new course record. The talent was there and so were a strong core of teammates, men like his brother Gordon, Mick Orton, George Johnson, and others.

They went down to Comrades after raising money with strip shows and concerts. Their junior man, Orton, won in a breakaway surprise and they finished 6th, 7th, 11th, 13th, 24th and 34th. "We were like kings," Bentley said fondly, the creases in each cheek deepening as he grinned. In 1971 he ran what still ranks among the ten fastest 100-milers ever (12:37:55). When the challenge of the 24-hour came up a year in advance, Bentley set to work running about 180 miles a week.

"I could never see myself not finishing," he said. "I settled down to run at an even pace."

"How did you handle it mentally?" I asked.

"I always thought about what I'd done, not what I was going to do. And I knew exactly what I wanted to achieve. I started drinking from the first mile and drank almost every lap after that. I drank 3½ gallons of accolade, and ate up 3½ pounds of glucose and three jars of honey, which I took off a jelly spoon every two miles. I also ate a dozen Milky Ways, custard jellies, soup and bread. I just walked fast when I was drinking but I wasn't going to come off like Wally Hayward. I knew I'd never get the record by resting. All your muscles ache but you're not so tired you have to stop. I was supposed to give urine samples to Dr. John Brotherhood but I cheated sometimes, just peed down my leg and sponged off later. I didn't want to take the time to stop. You know, by the end of the race all our urine was so bloody it was like black tea!

"There were several hundred people there near the end to push you on. Toward the finish I began to get more excited. I'd run all day and night in this white top but as I got close to being English native record holder I put my Tipton vest on. I went too fast, ate my food too fast, got too excited and I had trouble breathing. I also pulled a muscle in the right leg with about 3½ hours to go and it swelled up bang!—like that. After the record this leg went solid. I think it was the emotion—the mental strain had gone. Everyone kept shouting at me: Run! Run! But all I could do was hobble around, really. I was wobbling all over the place but no one could help me for fear of disqualifying me. Then I threw the blankets off and with only two minutes to go I was flying. Afterward I said to Ted Corbitt—he was just laying down—that was just a heat, the trial is tomorrow! I couldn't even move myself. We stopped in a pub that evening on the way home and I drank all the beer and ate all the sandwiches I could. I got back at 4:30 a.m., having been up for almost two days and I was in bed only two hours when the phone rang. It was a wonderful feeling really, although I threw away that last hour. I think it's a once-in-a-lifetime thing, running this kind of event, good to do at the end of your career."

It was obvious that the Tipton Harriers had thrived in a closely knit section of England, the area they call "Black Country," where pride in being tough and in the native sons who do well in sports is very strong. Among the friends who came down during the 24-hour race, Bentley said, was "one who was a cripple. He came out of the hospital, his wife drove him down and he got onto the track on his sticks, going round the whole way, shouting for me. That really lifted me, that did."

Not everyone can be an official champion. There just isn't room for more than one—not so long as people measure the differences in who went how far during 24 hours. It isn't the quality of the experience the outside world really cares about—or even the runner himself—but the quantity. Which isn't completely fair but then it doesn't really matter so much, perhaps, because not many remember what you did or when you did it anyway. Even the runners themselves sometimes have to struggle to recall the year or the time or the exact circumstances. What you've derived from it has sunk like water into dry soil, of value once but now half forgotten, never completely traceable.

One American who has tried his hand at such events is Ed Dodd, a frail-looking man at 5' 6" and 112 pounds. At the tag end of a February blizzard, I trudged down a row of modest brick-fronted homes in Collingswood, New Jersey, past knots of neighborhood boys who had hired themselves and their shovels out at 25¢ a head. Dodd, 33, a math teacher at a Catholic high school, came to the door with two of his three children bobbing along behind him. Together with his New Jersey colleague, Tom Osler, Dodd has delved deeply into a study of the 6-day races. They co-authored a monograph and then, later, a book on the subject of

6-day races and modern-day ultra training. Ed's 24-hour mileage counts don't put him at the top of the world list, but he has struggled as hard as anyone.

His wife Denise, a cheerful, unflappable sort who joined the conversation in between making dinner and keeping up with the two older boys and a seven-month-old daughter, said that all the ultrarunners they knew had good marriages. But then, she pointed out, "We knew what we were getting into. They're doing it strictly for themselves, for their own fun and pleasure. They're not out to make a name for themselves, but it's something—it's a goal. Ed has a lot of tenacity. I always remember when we got engaged a friend of ours came up and shook his hand and said, 'I congratulate you on your tenacity.' I didn't understand and then she said to me: 'I knew he'd wear you down. When he wants something he goes after it. He might not get a world class time but you can't change your body!'

"It does scare me to see him after some of these things. The worst time was last year after the December 24-hour at the Glassboro College [New Jersey] track. I'd had to leave at seven in the evening. They brought him in. I had never seen Ed throw up. He was shaking all over. He got a shower but when he got out he was trembling so bad he couldn't dry himself. I had to dry him off and I literally poured him into his pajamas and put him into bed. That was it! He wasn't going to run another one! I don't think he understood how bad he looked. Less than three weeks later he had a kidney stone attack. I sat in the hospital 24 hours watching him in utter pain. He didn't even know what he was doing."

The Dodds speculate that the dehydration of such a long run precipitated the attack. The stones attached to the inside of the kidney break off and travel down the urether, which causes extreme pain. It is a congenital condition and there is apparently always a risk of setting off an attack from the stress of a very long ultra.

The 24-hour runs strike Dodd as different in a way than the shorter road-and-track races he has run.

"Your emotional experiences, both the highs and the lows, don't seem to peak as high or dip as low as they do in the 24-hour runs. I never knew you could feel so depressed. There was one point in California where I had been out there 15, 16 hours, running one lap and walking one lap. I was sunburned and I hate the sun! I was exhausted, my legs hurt, I was nauseous and I thought: God, I've come 3,000 miles to get to this state—and quit and not even finish the race. I thought of all that training. Here I'd gone 14 hours and wasn't even two-thirds of the way done. I was a shambles. Later during the day, I finally snapped out of it. During the last half hour, when I knew it was just about over, I don't ever remember feeling that—I don't know if I had enough strength to be happy. I can't really describe it. It was an elation. A satisfaction. It was just incredible. Nothing, not even running in front of all those people at Boston running like crazy the last two miles, was nothing like finishing in front of 10 people when it was just getting light.

"I had special problems in California because of the sun. It was out the whole day. And it was still up there at 6:30 in the evening. I wasted a lot of energy and interest and excitement cursing the sun and sponging my sunburned arms and legs. It was a conscious effort not to use sunburn lotion, insane as that may sound. I was worried it would clog my pores and screw up my heating system. It was very bad sunburn I got. I had to go to the hospital and the doctor said my theory was just crap. In fact, he said, you would have to constantly reapply it because your sweat would wash it away. It was one of those little things . . . you go into a race and you think you've got all the bases covered. It was just the one thing I hadn't checked into. I hope I never run under those conditions again.

"I've learned something from 24-hour runs. I can certainly try anything I want to. I can give anything a good shot! Before, there may have been a lot of things I wanted to do but I would never even try because of being afraid I'll flop. A friend of mine told me in the October 24-hour run when I was in the doldrums, don't worry about what you do, just do your best. Which is my philosophy anyway. I've always done my best when I haven't tried to say, well, I'm going to win a race or break a record. I did this several times in college and always blew apart near the end. Some people need specific goals to go against. If you set a time limit, it's a really obvious failure if you don't meet it. But if you say you're just going to do your best, you've got a big out there. 'Well, did my best today! Too bad! Couldn't set the record.'

"Now I'm sure there are outer limits. I couldn't get up from a 24-hour the next day and do it again. But I wouldn't be afraid to try a 48-hour race or a 6-day race even. How did you do it, sleep 3 hours at a time? What intrigues me is that you don't know how to do it. Nobody does. So it's like you really are an explorer into new territory. You know, when I approach 24 hours now it doesn't seem that long a time actually. Six days does. It's all the mental set you make. It's confidence. You just tell yourself you're going to come out on the other side, just keep yourself on that track and things'll get better!"

3.
The Road and
Track Runs

One of the fastest men in the world over 50 or 100 miles is Cavin Woodward, whose character is a dazzling reversal of what one might expect from someone entitled to stack up first-place trophies and plaques for world-record times. The chipper confidence, the nuttiness, the burst of cackling laughter, the slight disdain for his rivals—all are signs that point to how the man at leisure in his home with his wife, Carol, and their three sons behaves on the roadways and quarter-mile tracks of his native England.

But only when the grayish-blue eyes behind his glasses turn sober as he discusses his attitude during races does another, topsy-turvy rationale for fueling his wins begin to emerge. It is not the glassy, aloof competitiveness of a Frank Shorter, or the up-front hunger for a win that pervades a Bill Rodgers. For Cavin Woodward clearly needs to put his back against the wall and talk himself down before he can feel free to attack back.

He is a sight to behold. In 1978 I saw him dueling head-on with Don Ritchie along M-106, the main motorway down to Brighton. His head cocked to one side, the look concentrated and unaware of what else was going on around him, the shortish legs lifting with a regular untiring action as his arms pumped fairly high above his chest, his hands flicking in a last final motion like the tail-end of a whip, and an audible hiss of air expelling from his lungs with each stride. He was like a small bull, undeterred by the lances stuck in him by fatigue. Men like Woodward don't drop out of races.

For the last few years, there has been a long shadow in his running career, and it is cast by the stooped, rocking-chair running gait of his most important rival, Don Ritchie. Ritchie has copped four of Woodward's four ultra world records. The two men are friendly enough when they meet, but they are relative strangers to one another and do not go off to local pubs to trade training secrets. Woodward is known for his low mileage. He is a reluctant trainer and, until recently, was what one might call an accomplished non-stretcher. In 1978, when I asked him whether he ever did any loosening up before a race, he looked at me with amusement. Such niceties, he said, he scarcely had time for. That seemed to me to be thoroughly English, no fanfare, no fanciness, no frills, no faddish American enthusiasms, just the old pound-and-sweat school of running, and I could hear an edge of pride in his voice which confirmed that was so. But in 1979, trouble with a chronically tight hamstring changed his attitude. He confessed that instead of toppling out of bed and out of the house for a 3- to 5-mile run, he now shaves first and *then* runs, so as at least to be on his feet a little longer. He runs between 45 miles (on a slow week) and 71 miles (on a good one), and races one place or another at almost any kind of distance just about every weekend. Without the races to look forward to, his training goes way down.

Just running the ultras that come up every season on England's busy calendar keeps him and his family dashing around, since their presence at races definitely matters very much.

Carol Woodward is sometimes called "the boss" by Cavin, when it comes to matters of training. She remembers his times and places at least as well as he does. For Cavin, many of the races blur into a general sort of memory. He credits his wife with making him first buckle down to it and start to run to win. Her encouragement worked. In 1975 at Crystal Palace, Cavin ran 100 miles in 11:38:54, shaving a neat 18 minutes off the old record, for a new world's best performance. En route to the 100 miles, he took the 100-kilometer record in 6:25:28. He followed that with a 150-kilometer record of 10:44:55. He has also won various ultra-races: the Epsom 40-miler; the Isle of Man 40; the Two Bridges 36-miler in Scotland and the Woodward-to-South End 40. Woodward is known for his fast starts. He likes to lead and he likes to run off as hard as he can from the beginning, hoping to break and demoralize the field behind. But he never runs relaxed.

"One of my qualities," he said, "is that I don't do anything that's risky. I've got to be sure before I make a move. You should never argue with me about what I've said, because I'm bloody sure it's right when I've said it. I'm proud of my consistency. Not many people in this country have run a hundred distance races [marathon or longer] in eight years. What I've proved and maybe people are starting to follow is that I always run the way people say you shouldn't, and that's fast from the start. I always slow down. I'm going to run successively slower, but I like to run my own race. I can slow down when I want, or speed up when I want.

Don Ritchie and Cavin Woodward hammer it out on the road to Brighton.

If you get in a bunch of four or five, you tend to do what everybody else does, don't you?

"I never expect to win a race. I can always find somebody that I think is going to beat me. It's good to be cautious, really, rather than say, oh, yeah, I'm going to win this. At the Isle of Man last year I did expect to win, but it was whether I could break the record. There's got to be something! The day before I found they'd extended the old course by half a mile. Anyway, I still broke the record. Or I expected to win the 100-miler *if* I could run 100 miles. In the Woodford to South End last year, a half hour before the start I learned Ritchie was there. So immediately I didn't expect to win it—I thought he would. I can always find somebody in the field who has beaten me. There's always reasons why. I think, well, I ran a 40-mile race the week before when they had a rest. I always find a reason. In Cornwall race I looked at the list and worked out that I was going to be about eighth. So long as I ran better than eighth, I was having a bloody good run, and as long as I felt that I ran a bit better. If you go in thinking you're going to win, and you're in eighth and they're getting away . . ."

"What will matter the most fifteen years from now?" I asked. "Or is it the day-to-day satisfactions that count?"

"On the day, the Isle of Man race last year gave me a great deal of satisfaction. On the day, I'd done something I'd always wanted to do. I went out there and I did it, I proved it, I achieved it. I was the favorite and I still did it. I suppose really the records are going to mean more to me in fifteen years' time than anything else. I've got a book there that tells me I did it and a silver platter over there . . ."

One of the fastest of the few women ultrarunners is Nina Kuscsik, the 40-year-old mother of three who hies from Huntington, Long Island, and is well known in U.S. road-running circles. Until the younger generation of women marathoners started beating their elders for top spots in the marathon classics such as New York and Boston in the past few years, the relatively older women like Kuscsik and Miki Gorman were top-ranked, not only stateside but on world lists. Kuscsik is hardly about to be phased out, however, and the big smile on her broad-cheeked face is still very much in evidence up near the top of the women's section in road races. In May 1979, she won the women's division of the difficult and hilly Yonkers marathon with a 3:03:56.

It seems a very distant time now but I can recall the first time I saw her race in the National AAU 50-Kilometer Championship, which was held on a stinking hot day in Vermont in 1973. The course meandered, in part, along a dirt road that rose and fell indifferently up and over the flank of one hippo-sided hill after another. With a few exceptions such as Natalie Cullimore, who was running 100 miles in 18 hours in California around that time, women just didn't try such things very often. Certainly Nina Kuscsik's own attitude was very low-key at the time, as she later explained:

"I just looked on it as a long excursion, the same way I looked on a marathon the first time I ran one. I felt if I ran well I would break the record—which I didn't—but the most important thing was to use it for training for the New York City Marathon which was a month later. By that time I had already broken 3 hours for the marathon, of which I'd run 12 already, so I was looking for a different experience and I found it. As a workout it did build me up, even though the temperature was 93 degrees.

"I was going through a difficult time in my life, and it turned out that the New York City Marathon took place four days before I was going to court to be divorced. With about 1½ miles to go in the marathon I started to get tight. I said, why not just pretend it's a 30-mile race? Okay, I thought, and I just relaxed. As long as I didn't think about that impending finishing line coming so soon, I was all right, and I ran a 2:57."

When I asked the reaction of other runners to seeing her as a woman in the 50-kilometer race, Kuscsik just shrugged.

"I don't know," she answered, in her strongly inflected New York voice. "I have a problem with that. My approach is that I'm a people, you're a people, we're all people doing this thing, so I don't give room maybe for people to express surprise or anything else. If they give me support and say, 'Oh, you did great!' well, I might give some back. It's a people thing—not man, not woman—and so very often I miss that whole feminist element. After the race Joe Kleinerman was giving out the awards and I was 17th. The awards went to 25 places, I think. I said, I don't want the first woman's award—I was the only woman—I want 17th place. I'm not sure what happened. The end result wasn't so important, it was just expressing what my feelings were."

No ultras followed for the next four years although in 1974 and 1975 she ran about 25 miles of the 50-mile race as a workout.

"I just wanted to watch it because it was so incredible," she said. "I thought it was just the end of the world to run that far."

Then, in 1977, she made the decision to run the whole race,

163

like so many others who never imagined initially they would try such a thing. The New York 50-Miler always starts early in the morning. Registration is at the old fieldhouse on 97th Street in Central Park, a rather shabby kind of place. There always seems to have been a heavy rainfall that first week in November, and you have to leap from one dry bit of flagstone to another to miss the massive puddles in front of the door. Outside, the runners sit on benches carefully swabbing Vaseline on their black-nailed toes, too tired to chatter very much. With slightly trembling fingers they fasten numbers to their shirts with safety pins. With ten minutes to go, like a den leader, a distracted-looking Joe Kleinerman, at last leads the motley pack over to the Park Drive, a three-lane roadway where stoplights continue to flash red and green, though motorists are barred for the day.

The 50-Miler starts in a nondescript place, at the top of a little rise. A few friends hold armfuls of sweats and wait to one side. Everyone waits. Under the gray sky conversation is subdued. When the gun fired in 1977, Kuscsik and 40 others trotted into motion.

"Eileen Waters had the record, something like 6:55, and when I started thinking about running it to break the record my plan was to run 15 miles, then walk a little bit, a real go-as-you-please type thing. Then, three weeks before, I heard that Judy Ikenberry had run 50 miles on the track in California in 6:44. I said, oh, there goes my walk. If I run well, I'll finish and if I'm not running well I don't want to finish. I decided I might as well enjoy the moment. I had a great time the whole way, partly because I was ahead of the record after 25 miles.

"I had an argument during the race with this guy, Benny, who was riding a bike in the park. I've known him for twenty years. It was before the 30-mile point, which was where I had decided I would evaluate myself, that he started riding alongside and telling me: 'You gotta keep going, you gotta finish no matter what, you gotta gut it out.' I said, 'Benny, I know my body, I know what I'm capable of.' 'No, you gotta do it,' he kept saying. I said, 'Benny, will you get lost!' Finally, he left.

"I didn't want any pacing during the race because if I was going to set a record I didn't want any questions raised about it. It was 9 loops and I figured if I could get my girlfriends to come out and ride their bikes and I go one loop with one, one loop with another—a loop is like 45 minutes—that's like a phone call, and I get to talk to all my girlfriends and the race will be over, but then I thought it might be like pacing so I didn't go with it.

"The race was on a Saturday. Thursday night I went out to a

restaurant with Bob Glover, because I had decided to join his team and we had a lot of things to talk about. We got the bill about 2:30 in the morning and it was quite expensive. 'We didn't eat that much,' I said. 'No,' they said, 'but you drank that much!' I got home at four in the morning, which was okay because I was off that Friday. I was so tired I didn't even manage to get to the store to buy soda and bananas for the race. I didn't think I would run anymore. But even though I tried to oversleep Saturday morning, I couldn't, so I came down and ran.

"The funniest part had to do with Paul Milvy, who ran the first 20 miles of the race and then went home to make lasagna because he was having a party that night. He came back into the park on his bike during my last loop. I guess he didn't really think I was going to still be running. 'You're still running! Oh, my God! Isn't that wonderful!' So he starts riding next to me. As we go into the bottom loop of the park, I said, 'Paul, when we get up to the East Side after 72nd Street, we're going to be pretty close to the finish and I don't mind if you ride with me then. But between here and there I want to just run by myself, because I want to enjoy this moment for what it is.' So he said, 'Okay,' and dropped behind, but it was just 30 feet and to everyone who passed he'd say: 'Isn't it wonderful!' I was happy that he was happy because it was just pure joy on his part that I was doing this thing, but meanwhile I didn't want to be aware of how wonderful it was. I just wanted to *feel* my body and not have to respond to outside stimuli.

"I'm a novice at ultras. I've run a lot of ultras in my head, but running a hundred miles in your head is not the same as running them on your feet! I think there's a certain mentality that can abide with ultramarathons. It's like Willie Mays said to me: 'I want to jog, I know it's good for me, but I can't stand it. I have to have instant results.' In ultras what you do in the first hour and a half is relatively unimportant, although it's very important in terms of pacing. When I ran the 50, at the marathon point, I felt I had run for just 5 miles. It was a tremendous feeling but it was proper pacing for what I felt capable of. I didn't have a single sore muscle like I always do after a marathon, but my joints were sore. It wasn't the distance I ran that bothered me but the time on my feet, the six and a half hours which was practically a whole workday. But I remember with 3 loops to go that 2 hours and 15 minutes seemed like nothing at all."

At the finish Kuscsik, who was then 38 years old, set the new American record for women of 6 hours, 35 minutes and 53 seconds, an average of 7 minutes and 50 seconds per mile. She was 14th among 20 finishers—41 had started.

A happy Nina Kusesik sets a new American women's record for 50 miles—6 hours 35 minutes 54 seconds.

4.
The Journey Run

Journey runners are a breed unto themselves. For the most part they join gladly enough in the usual ultraraces put on by their road-running brethren, but no sooner do they get some cash, a chance and a roadmap but they are off for open spaces. They string together a month or two or three of running 50 miles or longer a day. They meet the weather, the land and all the vagaries of chance that such an enterprise rains down upon them: rocky detours, stern highway patrolmen, savage dogs, rattlesnakes, sunburn, swollen ankles, thirst, dirty socks and the problem of where to spend the night.

The lucky ones have sponsors. Others, with nerves of ice and the indulgence of the gods, go off trusting to the turns of providence. These pilgrims specialize in any two spots on the planet separated by an unreasonable amount of distance. The grail that sustains them is first and foremost the dream of *sur*vival and *ar*rival. Certainly, like the others, they are greedy for records. Although the existential experience of following the changing vistas around them has its satisfactions, the old yearning to test oneself against the clock is often as not a big part of it.

Not always, however. Veteran journey hoofer John Ball of South Africa told a reporter recently why at the age of 52 he ran from Port Elizabeth to East London. He said, the run, which took him along 320 kilometers of unspoiled beach, was "marvelous."

He has done the run 5 times. "There's no traffic, away from everything," he said. "You can sort out problems. I was all right [after]—fit to live with again."

Journey runners simply know in a more grandiose way the satisfaction known to everyone who runs any distance. The irrefutable knowledge that you went from here to there offers the satisfaction of a certain precise accomplishment usually denied to other enterprises in life. Either you do what you set out to do or you do not.

Sometimes the fever may strike in a relatively modest way. Max White, a Virginia schoolteacher, lived in Charlottesville a few years back. His parents' home was in Richmond, 75 miles away. Casual queries by his students in a joking vein planted the idea in his mind. With the true journey runner's artistry, much as a woodcarver selects one piece of wood over another, White recalled later: "It was just a natural stretch. It was kind of tempting. It wasn't as if I was running into oblivion."

One morning he headed with his wife to their weekend morning run at the local track. There he announced he was running to Richmond that morning. Jenny said: "You can't just run there. That's something you have to plan for." He answered: "There's no way anyone would ever plan to run to Richmond." Later that day, his parents answered the door to discover their son, thirsty and tired, hoping for a reaction of delighted surprise. Like all parents, however they were more perturbed than pleased at such immoderation.

Other sons have done even more to turn their parents' hair white. From across the Atlantic comes a report on still another irrepressible Englishman, who took on one of the great feats in the progress of ultra pilgrims—a run around the world. Kelvin Bowers ran 10,289 miles in 18 months. In April 1974, he set out from Stoke-on-Trent accompanied in a white van by his wife Leona, their 2½-year-old son Zhenka, and two friends. In an account he later wrote, Bowers began:

> *To go out and run in one direction. Not ever going back over the same ground, but striding always towards an unfamiliar horizon.*
>
> *Shoes padding through tribal territories, stumbling across cobbled squares, lifting dust from deserts, and sending up flurries of snow from the stony tracks of isolated mountain passes. . . .*

After a ferry ride over the channel, Bowers ran down through various European countries, continuing on through Yugoslavia, Bulgaria and Turkey, where old women tried to roll rocks down into his path. Barry Bowler, a friend, joined Bowers in Turkey and continued on for the rest of the trip through Iran and Afghanistan. Bowers found the latter country a desolate place, "broken occasionally by nomadic encampments. . . Whenever they spotted us jogging by, whole families, accompanied by yapping hounds, would chase after us." The trek across Pakistan and India was followed by a sailing to Australia. From Perth they ran through "the endless bushlands of the outback" until finally reaching their goal, the steps of the Town Hall in Sydney.

Of all the great journey-run accounts, surely some of the most appealing to me are of those across America. Oddly enough, the runs have exerted the greatest fascination on the foreign-born, perhaps because a faint gold dust of fascination still clings to this continent. Not only is it a lovely shape designed for ocean-to-ocean, point-to-point running, it is also immense and filled with all manner of marvels and horrors, from sprawling urban freeways through deserts and over mountain ranges and along grasslands and farmlands and industrial centers. California and New York are, after all, the two mythic poles of the United States. Certainly the distance between them, about 3,000 miles, is just incredible enough to inspire, without being too completely far from reason. There is such a thing as an unofficial kind of record for a trans-U.S. run, but the obvious qualifications must be attached, to wit: that the course changes yearly as roads are straightened or phased in and out of existence. Further, there is no definite course, no overseeing body of journey runners to measure the route, to ask for proof that said applicant did on his or her own two feet actually do it, and so almost everyone who does the run covers a different distance. From the indefatigable Andy Milroy, the unofficial keeper of such records, I am indebted for the following list.

American Trans-Continental Progressive Records

John Ennis (US)
    80 days, 5 hours   NY–San Francisco, 1890
Edward Weston (US)
    77 days/3,483 miles   NY–LA, 1910
James A. Hocking (US)
    75days/3,754 miles   NY–SF, 1924
Don Shepherd (SA)
    73 days, 8 hrs, 20 mins./3,200 miles   LA–NY, 1964
Bruce Tulloh (GB)
    64 days, 21 hrs, 50 mins./2,876 miles   LA–NY, 1969
Marvin Swigart (US)
    62 days, 17 hrs/3,266 miles   SF–NY, 1971

John Ball* (SA)
    53 days, 23 hrs, 12½ mins./2,876 miles   LA–NY,
    1972
E. Gordon Brooks
    53 days, 7 hrs, 45 mins./2,876 miles   NY–LA,
    1974
Tom McGrath (EIR)
    53 days, 0 hrs, 7 mins./3,046 miles   NY–SF, 1977

The remarkable thing about Don Shepherd's run in 1964 is that the South African coal miner did it with a rucksack on his back with a few changes of clothing and odds and ends that he needed. He found water and food as he went, and by nightfall always managed to come up with a place to stay. Finally, he had to return each morning to the place where he left off in order not to cheat by a yard on having run the whole thing. So if he accepted a ride ahead to the next town from a passing motorist, he had to get back the next morning before being able to start again, a procedure that inevitably must have cost him some worry and time he might otherwise have devoted to running.

In the book he wrote later, *My Run Across the U.S.*, he comes across as a good-hearted fellow with a corny and undentable sense of humor about it all. He had practiced back home in a country which has produced its fair share of such runners. In the late 1950's he twice ran between Durban and Johannesburg, more than 410 miles, and another year ran from Johannesburg to Capetown, covering 910 miles in 23 stages at an average of 6 miles per hour. A friend accompanied him along the road on a motorbike. At one point, an old African man ran up to the friend, Piet Dooreward, and begged him not to abandon Shepherd on the road but to give him a lift. Dooreward explained that Shepherd wanted to run that way, but the old man didn't believe him. He shook his fist at Dooreward, saying (that "the Almighty would never forgive him for his cruelty.")

Bruce Tulloh, the Englishman, followed 5 years later with a

---

*The walking record is held by John Lees (GB), 53 days, 12 hrs, 15 mins./2,876 miles, LA–NY, 1972. The women's record is held by Mavis Hutchison, who was 53 when she took 69 days, 21 hrs, 40 mins. to go 2,871 miles, LA–NY, 1978.

carefully organized venture that turned out to be highly successful. He was sponsored by Schweppes, the bottling company, and his wife drove a support car along with one of their young sons. I had carefully read the fascinating little book Tulloh later wrote, *Four Million Footsteps*, one of the few running classics, which can only be found, it seems, in the Library of Congress. The "four million" refers to the presumed number of strides needed to carry this former Olympian on his immense journey.

Although I had carefully studied photographs of Tulloh during the run, it was one thing to remember the light grasshopper body burned brown from the sun clad only in shorts and shoes, and another altogether to match it up with any of the English gentlemen I saw gathered around the lunchtime offerings of a pub in Marlborough. Tulloh, who teaches grammar-school boys at the Marlborough School, had promised to meet me there for a bite of shepherd's pie. But there was no mistaking the slight, wiry man who came in dressed quite soberly in a schoolmaster's suit and tie. The face was thin and intense, and Tulloh began by answering questions with a fair degree of reticence. It seemed hard to imagine that so softspoken a person would have launched himself into such a zany enterprise, but by the time the afternoon had ended the answers to it were clear enough.

At one point, in spite of a chilling English downpour, I tagged along after the bounding figure of the former world-class 5,000-meter specialist on his way to coach some track runners. Everyone else at school had assumed the rain meant cancelation. Undaunted, Tulloh loped homewards. As he sat in his study reminiscing about the run and his yen for adventure, the controlled recklessness of his spirit shone through with an engaging boyishness. He had gone off to visit the Tarahumara for several weeks to run with them and see what they were like, more to satisfy himself than anything else. During a two-year stint at schoolmastering in Kenya with his family, he went off to Tanzania to visit a volcano that was supposed to erupt but, he added mildly, was just steaming instead. When the road ended, the safari party had to make do with imperfect maps on their way up to the summit of the volcano. "There were no mountain rescue teams or helicopters around that part of the world," Tulloh said happily. "No room for mistakes. It was tremendous fun."

Tulloh, whose track career coincided for a while with that of Ron Hill, the marathoner, had never been an ultrarunner, but in preparing for the trans-U.S. run he viewed it "as a closing chapter, as far as my own running was concerned. That sort of

Eleven years ago Bruce Tulloh ran across the U.S.
in 64 days 21 hours and 50 minutes.

173

long journey run does deaden your enthusiasm a bit. Your competitive instincts get really satisfied. I think it's the expenditure of adrenaline, planning it all, pushing yourself even when you're tired. It's not physical fatigue later. You just get used to running 50 miles a day but that mental drive to run in races left me."

A good deal of Tulloh's pleasure in the run seemed to be the organizational details that required straightening out, but he hardly neglected the psychological and physical preparation either. He went to visit Gavuzzi, "which had the benefit of showing me that one could adjust to the strain, because here I was meeting someone who'd done it. His advice was just to take it steadily and not try to go too fast."

"Were you particularly apprehensive before leaving for the U.S.?" I asked at one point.

"Well, I was ludicrously confident I would say. I did find in my training that when I first tried running consecutive 50-mile days it was very hard. It was a fairly soft record and I knew even if I did have some days I couldn't go very fast, it wouldn't be that hard to pick up the 45 or 50 miles a day needed to get ahead of the record. Nowadays to get the record you need to average about 55 miles a day. If you slip back you have to run a 60- or 70-mile day to make it up again, and that's when it really gets tough. I'd be much less confident about my ability to run it in 52 days because there's no room for mistakes. I figured if I had to walk I could do 35 a day and not lose too much.

"You know, I'm not really part of the ultra-distance scene. There's something far more exciting to me about running from one place to another than running 50 miles on a track. That would just bore me completely. I think in most cases the longer-distance men lack imagination. That's not meant as a personal criticism. It's just that I find the longer people run the quieter they are, the more dogged and stolid, the less imaginative. It does definitely require a different mental attitude than five- and ten-thousand-meter running. I think ultra men on the whole are mostly introverts."

Tulloh found getting from one side of the country to the other to be a feasible task, once his body was able to adjust to the daily strain. He spoke of getting on with the daily work as if it were more a question of logging in the time at a steady 8-miles-an-hour average, once the early injuries and patches of weariness faded away. He was too tired to do more than a minimum of stretching but never so tired that he forgot to eat. In fact, his normal food intake doubled so that despite his light, small frame, that was more ribs and kneecaps than anything else, he was packing in 6,000 calories a day. Vitamins were stowed in his luggage but used only once. His voice softened when he recalled one of the greatest daily pleasures of the run: "One of the nice things is being able to satisfy the tremendous thirst you've got at the end of the day and have some lovely six-packs of beer. Lovely!"

Tulloh felt in retrospect that most of what he learned on the trip tended to confirm his ideas and his sense of himself rather than presenting him with anything startlingly novel.

"Things become very much more simplified when you're doing something as simple and direct as that. It's very wearing emotionally. I found I would tend to laugh more and cry more perhaps because I was more tired, sandpapered down, think-skinned, all outer surfaces. You're much more susceptible. But having been running so many years I didn't think I was going to learn anything new. Although when you're out there with all that time ahead of you, it's a testing thing. You've got to be able to face it. I don't think you can become a long-distance runner unless you enjoy solitude. I very much enjoy company, but I don't find solitude oppressive at all. Running like that, there's not all that much solitude anyway since you meet people several times during the day. In a sense you're alone with your own ambitions. You've got to stay with that all the way across. You can't get away from that."

A more recent crosser is the current record holder, Tom McGrath, an Irishman living in New York City, who took on the journey at the age of 27 in 1977. I was among the small group of well-wishers who gathered in bright sunshine at the steps of City Hall in New York for the sendoff. McGrath, a small but stockily built Irish football player, had been in training for two years for the run. He had gotten married the day before to his childhood sweetheart. He set off smiling, holding an Irish flag in one hand and an American flag in the other. A few months later I went out to a bar in Queens to meet him for a chat about the run. When the door swung open and I glanced at the gaunt, mustachioed man I saw reflected in the doorway in the bar's mirror, I didn't recognize him as Tom McGrath. He acknowledged the searing physical and mental effort of getting through the run.

"I was on the road some days for 15 hours," McGrath said. "Running along I would just think about everything at all but I would try to keep in my head all the time the memory that I had a commitment to fulfill. There was no way I could stop. I'd wake up in the morning and be so sore and stiff I could just walk a few

Tom McGrath poses at the steps of City Hall
in New York with his wife, Mena, and Councilman Paul
O'Dwyer before leaving on a 1978 trans–U.S. run.

inches at a time. I often thought about how nice it would be when it was all over."

Certainly one of the greatest characters to ever strike out on the asphalt track across the States is Mavis Hutchison, the Galloping Granny from Johannesburg, South Africa, who was 53 when she completed her journey of almost 2,900 miles. It may have come as a surprise to readers of newspapers in thirteen states that a white-haired "old" lady was padding across their home territory on her way to becoming the first woman ever to go so far on a journey run, but it would not have caused an eye to blink in her native South Africa. The mother of four children who now range in age from 18 to 32, and the grandmother to seven, Mrs. Hutchison ran her first Comrades back in 1965. For that year and a few to come she was the only unofficial woman entrant who went out on race day.

She modestly referred to her first "real" long run as occurring in 1971 when, at the age of 46, she ran 106 miles, 736 yards in 24 hours, the former women's record. Remembering that it took place 6,000 feet above sea level makes her effort all the more praiseworthy. In 1973 she drew on her experience as a walker and covered 101 miles by that means in 24 hours. That same year she ran from Germiston City Hall to Durban, a distance of 602 kilometers, in 6 days, 12 hours and 55 minutes. The following year she ran the same course in reverse and took about a day longer because of the steep climbs up from the sea. In 1975 she ran from Pretoria, the government capital of South Africa, to Capetown, a 1,500-kilometer journey through the rugged veldt land to the tip of the country. That jaunt required 22 days and 4 hours. Finally, inspired in part by the examples of Don Shepherd and John Ball, she decided to give the trans-U.S. a go herself. A cosmetics firm, Vanda, put up the money, and with four friends and "Ern," her husband, she set off from Los Angeles City Hall in two campers—or, as they call them in her home country, caravans.

Mavis Hutchison, at 5′ 5″ and 108 pounds, hardly seems at first glance the tigress of the roads. She has a shock of snowy white hair, a strong face and a soft voice, which often seems at odds with the *sturm und drang* of her journey runs. Her storytelling is hypnotic, if exhausting after a point, for she can turn a run across the dilapidated bridge of a midwestern city into a slippery tug of war between the forces of survival and capitulation. She makes no attempt to present herself as an iron woman. In fact, she states, if she learned anything of value on the trip, it was that someone as ordinary and fearful as herself—afraid, as she put it, to talk to strangers or to learn to drive a car—could adjust to and eventually overcome the biggest challenge of her life. She did not paint herself either in false colors, making it clear that she had her own way of adjusting to the rigors of the run by remaining quiet and private, while her support crew had to struggle with the tension of a 2½-month slow boat journey overland.

"Now I can assure you when I lined up in front of Los Angeles City Hall at nine o'clock in the morning I was so nervous I was honestly terrified. I thought to myself, what are you doing? You know, originally my sponsor had asked me to withdraw because of the political business with South Africa, and I would be a sitting target for anybody. But I knew if I withdrew I might never get the opportunity again. Still, it was a fantastic chance to opt out. Everybody would have told me it was the right thing. When I thought of the 70 days ahead of me . . . my mind couldn't accept it, my mind was too small. But imagine if I had told these five people, now we've had enough, let's go home. I don't think I would have done it, but I was terribly tempted because I had a feeling that this time the task was bigger than I was.

"Of course the first day was lovely. I did 35 miles, which I had planned on. Once I got on the road I felt all right. I knew! It was amazing but I knew I was going to get to New York. All that tension had been released, and from then on at no time did I ever doubt that I was going to get there. But there were times I assure you when I didn't know how I was going to get through the day or even the next hour. Some American friends who were out here in 1976 for a Masters track and field meet and also in Sweden in 1977 ran the first 25 miles with me.

"It took two days of running to get out of Los Angeles. Then I got my first upset. I wasn't allowed on the freeways so I had to take a detour of 39 miles, virtually a whole day I was giving away. Palm Springs. Mecca. Box Canyon. Big, huge red mountains. It was isolated and lonely. We had two motorized caravans, but we were told it wasn't safe to sleep on the side of the roads where I would finish each night, so we went off to trailer parks. That meant quite a bit of traveling every morning and evening. Sometimes I was on the road at four in the morning until eight o'clock at night. I remember one detour on a narrow road that was filled with boulders and stones and little bushes, just ditches on the side, really. I was terrified of hurting myself. I had to watch every step so carefully. Then after that came a beautiful road. I wouldn't worry too much about what lay ahead of me, and no point in worrying about what's behind me, that's finished. I'd try to concentrate on the present. That was the only thing that was important, the only thing I had to get through at the time. I honestly believe that if I'd had to contemplate this enormous distance ahead of me all the time, I would never have been able to see it through. Seventy days is almost three times what I'd done.

"Some of those truckers got to know me after two or three weeks on the road, during their hauls up and down. One trucker stopped and said to Lucy, 'Look, this is the third time I've seen her in three weeks.' He said, 'What is she doing on the road, surely she's not slimming?' Another trucker stopped to find out what I was doing and said to Ern, 'Well, I salute her. Here's a cigar for you and one for her!' I still have it. Basically I found the American people very warmhearted. They were very interested but none of them ever thought I would get to New York. I think when they saw this white hair they really couldn't conceive it. Although once I got past the halfway stage, you could feel the change from 'is she going to make it' to 'she's going to make it.'

"My handlers had to put me on some detour around a town once, because of construction and washaways, and eventually there were so many detours there was no road anymore and I was running in a riverbed. I was upset because it seemed all for nothing. It was two or three hours I was losing, so they said, well, never mind; if you like we'll record this extra mileage and give you a lift to the main road. I said, 'Thank you very much, but if there is a shortcut I will take it on my own two feet.' I was so cross with them!

I was terribly conscious of the tension they were all under. When they'd say come off the road, I'd come off. Once or twice I'd argue and say I'd like to stay on another hour, there's too much good light to waste, but they were under terrible strain. Can you imagine what it is like to sit virtually in a caravan for 70 days? They got bored and were sometimes losing interest. I begged them to take a break and do a bit of sightseeing. Amazingly, for the first 21 days everything was fine. It was after that then that I could feel the tension but there was nothing I could do.

"I found the pollution on the roads unbelievable in America. Honestly, I picked up enough good tools along the side of the road to equip a whole workshop, but it was just a hundredth of what was there. I gave everybody a hat. I saved a dozen pens, knives, a big hacksaw which I ran with for about two miles but it was too heavy so I threw it down. I saw a chess set but I didn't take time for it because I would have had to count to see if it was complete.

"Going through New Mexico there was such a strong wind it just about blew me off my feet, and when these trucks came past they were so big and heavy. And what with their suction they pulled me and threw me a couple of feet ahead. They used to be quite fascinated in the caravans sitting there watching the trucks throw me around!

"On the highway out west once, a car pulled off to the side of the road and a little couple, probably on holiday, got out. They wanted to know what was going on, so Ern explained. So she said to her husband, 'I think you'd better take her photograph, she may just become famous.' So he duly did that and when he finished she said to her husband, 'Now give the gentleman a dollar!'

"Some of these cars would stop, and if it was a man all he'd do was open the passenger door. I don't know if he thought I was going to slide in as I ran past or what. I didn't have the heart to just run past so I'd stop and say, 'Thank you very much, but I'm just running to that caravan over there." 'Then I'll give you a ride there,' they'd say. No, I'm doing a marathon—I wouldn't say what it was—just I'm doing a marathon. Sometimes they'd think I just didn't like them. You could see by the way they slammed the door and pulled off. A couple of truckers got out to offer me a lift, as if I were a damsel in distress. They walked around the truck as if they were examining the wheels and when I went by they'd say, 'Hop in.' I'd say, 'Sorry.' Some looked embarassed, others got annoyed. They often thought I was genuinely in trouble.

"On the 25th day we entered Texas. My right leg was beginning to ache a bit. I thought to myself, well, you just keep on and it will go away. Just pretend it's not there. When I'd come off the road I used to doctor it, massage it and so on, but I didn't want the rest of them to know so I carried on. In Oklahoma a week later, my leg really gave trouble. One morning I was bundled up against the cold and went out but just couldn't lift the foot up after four steps. I didn't run at all that day. It was the hardest day I spent. The next day all I managed was 33 miles. I had shin splints and was in tremendous pain. It felt like someone had taken a red-hot poker and was pushing it up and down, and that this metal band around the leg was getting tighter and tighter.

"On the 41st day we went into Missouri. We went through East St. Louis, a poor black area, which only later did we learn was supposed to be terribly dangerous. But we didn't know and everyone there was very nice to us. All these teenagers came up and said, didn't we see you last night on TV? They shook my hand and were very nice indeed.

"I had one very bad day in Ohio. By eleven o'clock that morning I felt I had had enough and I just couldn't carry on. I only knew I had to carry on. That's all that kept me going. I was mentally, spiritually and physically exhausted. I felt as if I was crawling. I just didn't care. But by three o'clock that afternoon I felt as if I'd broken that barrier and I knew then the rest of the day wasn't going to be as bad.

"All my meals I had by myself. At night I'd rest for an hour or so before eating. The only reason I ate was because I had to; I didn't really feel like it. When the other two ladies were ready to go to sleep, they came in and I would already be asleep. They left me alone most of the time. The pain was so bad for a while at night that it felt as if my leg were curling up. It would keep me awake and my feet ached. I took two aspirins every night. When I think about it now I can't really credit that I could bear with it. At times I wanted to say, please God, take this pain away, but I knew it wasn't going to help so I just said, please God, give me the courage to bear this pain.

"There are all these cracks in the road in America, so all I'd do sometimes was concentrate on getting from this crack to this crack and then to the next. It's surprising how a whole day can go like that. You can bear pain for one day, not for 20 or 30, so you had to just bear it for that day. And the next you start completely afresh. When I got to 22 days, that was as long as my longest previous run, so all I had to do was go for another 22 days and then another.

"On the 54th day we got into Ohio and the rains started every day, but hours tick by whether it rains or not. I had no option. I had to go on. I had now got to the stage that whatever the circumstances were, I was prepared to accept them. It didn't matter. I was running better and getting better mileages. My attitude had sorted itself out. Near the end of the trip we passed a hitchhiker who was tired after walking two miles. He was lying down on the side of the road with his head on his pack thumbing a lift!

"The day before getting to New York on the 18-mile New Jersey stretch to the Verrazano Narrows bridge, I was walking backwards sometimes around bends to keep an eye on traffic. The next morning they closed the bridge down for me and the runners who were taking me in to the finish. I was terribly nervous that I was going to be late, but we were ahead of schedule so we had to stop occasionally and kill time. We ran over the Brooklyn Bridge, they said turn here and *there* was the City Hall. I wasn't prepared to see it so soon. I got a medal, a bowl, flowers. Then some TV people came and asked can I do it again. So I did. But when it came to the 6th pose for each set of cameras I was terribly embarrassed.

"When all this was over I had the most tremendous feeling. I had achieved the ambition of a lifetime. I'd actually done it. It was quite something. The next day the number-one thing in my life was to have a haircut! But when I woke up I realized, I've still got a lifetime ahead of me. What I've done is now completed. There's another challenge, another hill ahead of me which I probably have to prepare myself for. It just doesn't end, it just goes on until one day you're not there to go on. I want to go in twenty directions all of a sudden. You plan ahead for ten years or a hundred years but you move slowly, one day at a time. From the terribly negative sort of person I was all my life has come so much in the running that is worthwhile to me. At the start of the run across America, I knew all I had to do was one step at a time. Years ago if anybody had asked me to speak to a stranger, I would have run a mile. To speak to my own family was enough. I probably had to be that kind of person. You yourself are your own handicap. A lot of us have disabilities to which we readjust—that's what I feel."

183

Joe Erskine gets a drink during the 1979
Two Bridges race in upstate New York.

Legendary Ted Corbitt, America's foremost ultrapioneer, takes a lunchtime run by the East River.

5
ON THE RUN AT HOME AND ABROAD

1.
In America

On the map of New York State, Route 9 hugs the eastern shore of the Hudson River. It is a classic north-south route of endearing simplicity for professional map-readers and wanderers. Not too far out of New York City, say twelve miles or so, is a small luncheonette called Bob and Milly's. Bob, a man in his early 50's, has been working behind the counter for years. He has seen them all come in—the wanderers, that is, the loons, drawn as helplessly by the track of Route 9 going north as birds by their migratory instincts.

"You fellas want ice water?" he asks knowingly. In that simple hamburger joint, he has seen all the greats. Ted Corbitt, John Garlepp, Steve Grotsky, Jim McDonagh, the vets and the yearlings. They must all look pretty much alike to him, shining with sweat and their own stink, fishing limp dollar bills out of their shoes or from a safety pin that keeps the money fastened to their shorts. Still American currency, wet or dry, is legal tender, and so Bob flattens out the payment for the Cokes and 7-Ups and milk-shakes, and shakes his head at the Saturday appearance of the boys.

This is pretty much where it all started in the United States back in the late sixties, when a few of the fellows got it into their heads that they would like to try such things. They are still around, still interested for the most part in ultras, whether or not they themselves run anymore. Ted Corbitt, who never quite seems to give up hope that he can overcome chronic injuries and asthma to hit the road again, works as chief physical therapist at the Institute for the Crippled and Disabled in lower Manhattan. He sometimes gets calls from local ultrarunners like Rich Langsam, or the out-of-town supplicants like Don Choi, who know that this quiet man knows an immense amount about how to treat athletic injuries.

Unfortunately, a lot of what Ted learned came about through personal experience. His running career has been plagued with various rips, tears and strains, as well as the kind of accidents that would be laughable if they were not so terrible. In one race, a sock slipped down an overly Vaselined foot and bunched up at the front of his toes, causing his feet to cramp. Corbitt debated whether to stop and lose time or just let it go. Characteristically, he let it go and struggled on.

Corbitt was born in 1920 and raised in his early years in rural South Carolina, where he ran to school every day. At high school and later at the University of Cincinnati, he was a promising sprinter, running the 440 in less than 50 seconds. After college his training was erratic, and not until he was about 30 did he begin serious marathon training. He scoured the little material there was to be found about such things in the New York public libraries. Some of his techniques—such as running through the streets of New York with combat boots to strengthen his legs—were typical and early signs of his willingness to push hard. By 1952, Corbitt had qualified for the Olympic Games in the marathon at Helsinki, where he placed a disappointing 44th, hampered the entire way by a bad sidestitch. It was, as he put it later, just a way station.

His running career continued with a heavy emphasis on marathons. During that time ultrarunning was unknown in the United States. Corbitt and marathoner Aldo Scandurra emerged as the prime pushers for the first revival of ultra distances in this country since the demise of the wobbles. In 1959 the Amateur Athletic Union (AAU) agreed to sponsor an RRC 30-miler in the Bronx. From 1962 on, ultra races began to crop up more occasionally on both the East and West Coasts. And in 1966, with the indefatigable Scandurra as chairman, the AAU Long Distance and Road Racing Committee wrested approval for a 50-mile race that would be the national championship.

In 1958 Corbitt was among the founders of the American RRC and became its first president. Browning Ross, of the British RRC, had encouraged Corbitt to take a role in getting the novice organization under way. The New York RRC went on to become a powerhouse sponsor of a number of fine marathons and ultras. Like all such organizations, a few people did all the work on their kitchen tables and knew each other by first names. Such a thing was possible in the winter of 1966, when membership was still only 139. In the fall of 1979, the New York RRC had over 11,000 enrolled!

As Corbitt got older he showed no signs of slowing down. He ran the Brighton 5 times and took second 3 times. He was just about alone in the entire city in training at such tremendous lengths. Buildups for the Brighton meant struggling through the steambath of New York City in July and August. One year he ran over 100 miles nonstop in practice on a weekend. Another time he ran around Manhattan twice—a good 62 miles. One July he ran 1,000 miles. Dogs bit him. Injuries frayed his patience and his tendons.

When Corbitt was 49 years old he flew to England for the Walton-on-Thames 100-miler, where he took third place in 13:33:06 (1969). At the age of 53 he returned to run Brighton in his best time to date, and then stayed on a few more weeks to run the Walton-on-Thames 24-hour. There were 3 good hours, but the closing 21 were what he still terms ten years later "a nightmare." The first hour was smooth; the second hour was a "tremendous" high, which to this day he still does not understand. It felt like the best running of his life, but by the end of the third hour, inexplicably, deep pain began to bite into his thighs. Sustained until about the 17th hour by the hope of running through it, Corbitt finally just had little left to hope for but the knowledge that if he just continued he would ultimately be able to stop. A torrential downpour of chilling rain near the end of the run, which left the track awash in water for a while, was "mind-blowing." He still managed to go 136 miles, 782 yards, which remained the American record until 1978 when Don Choi ran an unofficial 136 miles, 716 yards.

For such an accomplished nontalker, Corbitt has cast a very long shadow in the world of ultras. He is the daddy of modern ultrarunning in this country, and the near 200 marathons and ultramarathons he has covered so far since 1951 have taken on epic scope. It must have seemed mighty lonely at the time as he pounded along with his awkward, splay-footed, steeped-in-agony running style: down from his home near the tip of Manhattan along the upper reaches of northern Broadway; through the neglected wilds of hilly Inwood Park; along the West Side Highway and on to Riverside Drive, where from the open stretch of bridge north of Grant's Tomb he could look out over the tar roofs of the wholesale butchers eighty feet below to the far sweep of the Hudson River. And on down into the dense traffic of central Manhattan on his way to work, dodging cars and ignoring the curious. He wonders now if all the years of running in polluted streets didn't damage his lungs, bequeathing him his current respiratory problems. Nor could the incessant pounding over concrete and asphalt, and the pushing, pushing, pushing through the outer reaches of will and aching joints, help but leave him with a sore hip and shortened stride.

Corbitt is the kind of man you get to know easily and yet not very well at all. With most people, he simply doesn't know how to make small talk. His voice level is just above a mumble, but there is a kindliness and delicacy to his manner that everyone senses. There is just something special about the man. He makes people feel he might do anything he sets his mind to, but he makes no claims for himself although he talks freely enough about his races if asked. Go to him for advice about an injury and he gives up his lunch hour to examine the problematic leg. And when the petitioner looks to thank Ted or to offer a payment (that will never be accepted), he will have vanished on the soft, rubber-soled shoes which bear him noiselessly about among the halted and lame and congenitally deformed folk who troop through his domain.

It is affecting in a way to sit there, watching the grand master of the roads, the dean of extreme sustained movement, with his thin black arms and delicate fingers manipulating the legs and arms of his patients, who would be happy enough just to walk easily, let alone run. Corbitt has been trying for the past few years to regain a measure of his old form, and he works carefully with diet, with podiatrists and other specialists, following the same relentless search for the right treatment that so many ultrarunners have followed, with their ragged list of chronic problems.

Corbitt has been consistent in a sport that wears people down. It is easy to train hard for a while, but sometimes, when I come back from a tiresome workout and wonder how many more years I will go with it myself, it seems not very surprising to me that people give up training hard and racing hard. The love for it has to burn very deep, but judgment matters too, where mere tenacity or greed will destroy.

"I've seen some fine ultrarunners get overexcited," Corbitt said once. "They think if they run a hard 100-miler they can just go out and do anything they want. It doesn't work like that. You have to back away sometimes. And there's a lot of information around that people don't take advantage of about diet and training and building up strength. When you're young you can eat whatever you want, do a lot of things that push the limit, and you just can get through most of it. But if you want to go on when you're older and your body juices are literally drying up, it's not so easy."

Such prehistory matters little to anyone right now. Nat Cirulnick, a Queens schoolteacher who has been one of the regulars from way back when, mentioned to me casually at a race that he had some early copies of his short-lived attempt to compile and sell an "Annual Marathon Guide." These cheaply printed roundups referred to ultras as "super marathons," since no other term seemed appropriate. Like an anxious bloodhound in search of a bone, I stood by in the garage of his home in Rosedale waiting for this publication of long ago to be brought to light. When Cirulnick unearthed it, I saw that several races were listed for 1963 with Corbitt's name at the top and two to four other names listed for the entire roster. They would all pack into a single station wagon and drive off to the start together.

One of the survivors of those long past days is John Garlepp, whose rise and fall into fitness and out of it has a long-term cycle of its own. Garlepp can usually be found of a summer Saturday morning in the subway car barn of the New York Transit Authority, up at Van Cortland Park in the northernmost reaches of the city, where he's prepared for the London–Brighton race or the New York 50 since his early 20's. There, amidst the cavernous gloom of the old building where he works servicing subway car motors, he changes into his running clothes for a run up Route 9 with a group comprised mostly of ultra yearlings. His muscular arms and torso are a reminder of the middleweight Golden Glove finals he was a part of back in 1957, in his late teens.

"Aldo Scandurra was one of the people who helped ultrarunning along at the very beginning," Garlepp said. "He would organize these races at Alley Pond Park and bring out a lot of water and fruit juices.

"For years he and Ted were the backbone of the movement. As far as training, I don't think anybody knew what the hell was going on. Jim McDonagh did over 200 miles a week consistently. That was his secret, though he would never admit it.

"My first ultra was the only race that Ted didn't run, and I won it. It was supposed to be a 45-miler but it was around 41 point something. I got into trouble with stitches, so I lay down on the side of the road and tried to do some situps since I heard that helped, but I was so sore that I couldn't. I had to roll onto my stomach and get onto my knees before I could get up. It was weird. I also had this tremendous urge to lay down and go to sleep. But I ran a good time and nobody could believe it. It was supposed to be a qualifier to go to the Brighton race, but I didn't even realize what the heck was going on. And there I was, supposed to be the fastest guy going to England. I really didn't believe it until a week before we were supposed to go.

"I never let any distance faze me. I went to England, got on the line, the gun went off and, bingo, I went off with this Englishman. And I went through 20 in under 2 hours. I didn't even remember the course the first year we ran it.

Allan Kirik wins the Knickerbocker
60-kilometer, New York City, 1979.

"With all these marathon runners we have in the States nowadays the fields are definitely going to grow in ultras, but it's going to take a few years. We haven't even scratched the surface."

The happy-go-lucky generation of such pioneers is not entirely over. Garlepp still races. So does Gary Muhrcke. McDonagh is back home in Ireland. Cirulnick is always out there, though he has slowed considerably compared to his previous times. There were not too many more than those. The seventies brought some new faces who are now the ones to reckon with, although the last three years in particular have seen faster men and women pop up who were not around before.

There were brief, meteoric flashes in the constellations in the early seventies. Jose Cortez, as a mere stripling of 19, ran what is still the top-ranked 100-miler for Americans: a 12:54:31 in 1971 at Rocklin, California. Although I have never met Cortez, I wonder if his freshness to the whole thing was not an immense advantage—perhaps he simply went ahead and ran it as best he knew how. In that same race Natalie Cullimore, who was then 35, chalked up what is still the American women's fastest 100-mile time: 16:11:00. A few other folk tottered around and around various tracks with decent times—Ralph Paffenbarger who was in his late 40's, and Paul Reese who was in his early 50's.

In the mid-1970's, runners like Max White, Jim Pearson, and Park Barner came into their own. White won some ultraraces on the East Coast with fast times, and shone out in his single Brighton performance to date, probably running one of the fastest 50-milers ever for an American en route to the finish, although no 50-mile split is taken at Brighton. Since then White, who teaches math, turned his attention to running marathons in the low 2:20's, although he is about to resume his ultra career again. He has the speed, the tenacity and the boundless energy to put him back among the top rollers once more.

Jim Pearson, another schoolteacher, lives out in Bellingham, Washington, where ultrarunning is a more thinly populated sport than in California or the northeast of the United States. Until 1979 the easygoing Pearson held the official American 50-mile road record with a 5:12:41. That has since been taken away by the tow-headed, mustachioed Allan Kirik, whose shuffle-along style propelled him in grand form to a 50-mile posting of 5:00:30 in 1979 at Lake Waramaug, Connecticut. That is just over 6-minutes-per-mile running, a very fine achievement.

Today there are perhaps a couple of dozen runners around the country who rank near the top, of varying but undoubted ability.

Abe Underwood, Rich Langsam, Ken Moffitt, Frank Bozanich, Peter Monahan, Jim Gallup, Darryl Beardall, Bill Lawder, Joe Erskine, Roger Welch, Stu Mittleman, Tom Osler and Cahit Yeter are the men in this group, many of them ranging in age from their late twenties to their late forties. The women include Ruth Anderson, Sue Ellen Trapp, Lydi Pallares, Sue Medoglia and Marcy Schwam. Schwam set the former women's record for 24 hours with a 1979 distance of 113 miles, 1,183 yards. This was en route to running 146 miles in a 48-hour race! Trapp now holds the 24 hour record with a pending 1980 world record mark of 125 miles, 675 yards.

Occupations vary. An unusually high number work with numbers. There are math teachers (Dodd, Osler, White) and an accountant (Langsam). Pat Burke is an elevator mechanic, Yeter is a saucier, and Erskine is a crane operator. There are the occasional speedsters in marathons who show up once or twice for a race such as tall, fast-talking salesman Paul Fetscher, fireman-turned-runner store merchant Gary Muhrcke, and research chemist Fritz Mueller, who is best known for his 2:21 marathon time at Boston at the age of 41. There are the stalwarts, such as red-bearded, freckle-skinned, crinkle-eyed Jerry Mahier, who is one of the tireless perennials at the 50-miler in New York; and plod-along John Kenul, who can always be counted on to finish—often last, but never discouraged. Each one knows most of the others, and they all are distinct cameo personalities, unmistakable one from another.

Lawder is the running fanatic, who flies to England, or Miami, or down to Virginia or wherever, to gobble up as many ultra and marathon runs as he can, frequently running the latter in 2:40-plus time simply as a workout. Langsam, an accountant in midtown Manhattan, will run around the island once in a while to stay in trim, and he's frequently needled by his friends for his predilection for skimpy Union Jack shorts and European-cut racing tanktops.

Pat Burke, a transplanted Irishman, gets his mind off the hard parts of a race by recalling the country lanes and fields he walked through as a boy. He has wiry black hair brushed straight back and a pair of white-skinned knobby-kneed legs that are famous for carrying him to work from his New Jersey home into midtown Manhattan and back again at the end of the day, a good 40-mile workout. He often invites friends to sample the heat of the boiler-room area where he spends many of his working hours, asserting that it's good preparation for summertime racing. Burke is known among comrades as an overly zealous workhorse, whose nagging bouts of sciatica are most likely due to his appetite for training hard.

Osler, who is beginning to push 40 years of age, is a little bit removed from immediate contact with the New York–New England connection. A recurrent battler of extra weight, Osler has been involved in running for a long time. He is responsible for much of the revived interest on the national scene in 24-hour runs, having put on a couple of such efforts himself on a rutted cinder track in his hometown of Glassboro, New Jersey. A group of local crazies, taking heart from his example, tried 100-milers, 24-hour runs and 12-hour efforts, all put on in $5-budget, do-it-yourself style where participants, in a touching display of faith in human honesty, are held responsible for counting each of their laps on a hand-held counter which they provide themselves.

One wintry night, I arrived at 3 a.m. at the Glassboro track to greet a whiskery Osler. He had retired from the race after some scores of miles and was lounging around in his long underwear and watch cap as comfortably as other men sport a three-piece suit. Meanwhile his colleague, Ed Dodd, limped around under the skimpy arc lights, blanket over his shoulders, resembling nothing so much as a Civil War veteran.

The runner who comes nearest to replacing Corbitt in mythic proportion is 35-year-old Park Barner. Barner, who works with computers for the state department of revenue in Harrisburg, Pennsylvania, is not daunted by much. Not a great talker, he's never inclined to spill his heart out to an interviewer. Instead he discusses his efforts reasonably in a low-key kind of way, although he makes no pretense of not enjoying the notoriety running has brought him—a story in *Sports Illustrated*, the fame of one of the longest 24-hour efforts in history to date, and the knowledge that he is certainly the best-known ultrarunner currently on the roads.

He may not be the fastest, especially at the shorter distances like 50 miles or 100 kilometers, but he always gives the impression that if he were to put his mind to it, he could escalate the ante out beyond anybody else's reach. Park runs with little visible strain and can do so for hours and hours at a time. Others may run more quickly, but none as yet have gone so far for so long.

He lives at home with his parents in Enola, a small town on the other side of the Susquehanna River, an area dominated by the shadow of the recession which blighted the growth of the nearby railroad yards (the largest in the world) where his father once

After setting an American record for 100 kilometers,
Park Barner enjoys the sensation of standing still.

worked. Undaunted by the nuclear fallout from nearby Three Mile Island in the spring of 1979, Barner was one of a few who insisted on plodding through a Harrisburg 100-kilo race, which out-of-state ultrarunners avoided like the plague.

Barner doesn't train phenomenal amounts, and he's been interested in other sports—he once considered a career as a pro bowler. He trains mostly on his own. If his bearded friend, Nick Marshall, ultra statistician supreme, and a resident of a neighboring town, wants to get in touch with Barner, he simply runs out to join him along his set path to work. Or, rather he used to do so, since Marshall's long streak of consecutive running days came to a halt in 1979 when injuries sidelined him, perhaps for good. He never ran an ultra easily after a hard effort in the 1978 100-miler.

Barner's reputation first began to spread when people on the sidelines would point to him as he strode past, saying disbelievingly that he was going to "double" that weekend—that is, run a 50-miler on a Saturday and a marathon on a Sunday, or vice versa. Practice in doubling has paid off. In 1978, on the frozen Glassboro track where he set a new, unofficial American record of 152 miles, 1,599 yards, he quaffed 11 quarts of liquid including water, Gatorade, orange juice and coffee. I wasn't surprised to hear that he ran with only a T-shirt and shorts to cover his 170-pound-plus frame. A year earlier, during a 100-kilometer race in Mechanicsburg, Pennsylvania, he rolled on past me on the loop course looking like some giant bat, as the sharp wintry wind filled his half-open nylon shell and riffled his neon-colored shorts. His massive thighs had broken out into goosebumps, but Barner wasn't cold, although I, for one, was a soaked and chattering rat. Following the 1978 24-hour race, he catnapped for two hours and drove on to Maryland to run in a 50-mile race the next day.

As a marathoner with a personal best of 2:37:28, Barner moved up to ultras about 1972 and has put most of his effort into them ever since. He is near the top of the list for Americans in the 100-miler (13:40:59), a performance set in 1975 on a broiling August day at Queensboro Community College in New York. He has won numerous 100-kilometer races and for five years held the American record, pushing it down to 7:11:44 until Frank Bozanich, a Marine officer, hammered out a 6:51:21 on a sweltering day in Miami, Florida in early 1979.

In 1974 Barner entered the Chesapeake and Ohio Canal race, which covers 300 kilometers of abandoned towpath between Washington, D.C. and Cumberland, Maryland. This race, which at present has not been staged for several years, was scheduled for three 1 day stages of 100 kilometers a day. The first year it was held there were no finishers. The second year Barner's total elapsed time was 23:53:34, with 100-kilo splits of 7:52:43, 8:12:34 and 7:48:17. Out of the 6 other entrants, only one completed the course. The next year found Barner back at the starting line with a startling idea in mind—he would run nonstop the entire distance, compressing the three stages into one. Needless to say, no one had ever run the race *that* way before. The flat roadway skirts the edge of forest and field but is isolated and lonely at night, since no access roads cross its path and motor vehicles are prohibited. The race began with a slight headwind and a temperature in the 40's, but well into nightfall the thermometer plunged to 18 degress Fahrenheit. The roadway had crumbled and eroded away in sections, forcing Barner to ford a couple of waist-deep streams. Barner finally got cold and the consequences could have been disastrous.

"It was just after dark," Barner said later, "and I noticed frost on the leaves. Up till then I hadn't noticed it was that cold. When I met Al Somerville at 81 miles, I put on an extra T-shirt and sweat pants. I thought that was all that I'd need. I guess I wasn't running fast enough to generate heat, which I was losing all night. Finally, about four in the morning, it really hit me. I just had the feeling that I had to lay down and go to sleep, even though I was in the middle of running. It was almost overpowering. I'd stop and bend over but it really made me sleepier.

"I lost focus. The towpath was like a gravel road, with tire tracks running through the sides and a little grass in the middle some places. Say there'd be a puddle on the left side and I'd be running on the right side. Next thing I'd be on the other side trying to keep out of the way of the puddle! I was just falling asleep on my feet. Luckily I was getting close to where Bob Crane and Al were going to meet me. I knew the danger from hypothermia. Once you stop . . . if I'd laid down, cold as I was and cold as the night was, that would have been it. I hate to think of that.

"Anyway, once I got in the car they had the heater running and I napped for about a half hour. But when I warmed up I started shivering. Once I started running again I felt like I was just starting out fresh."

Barner's total elapsed time, including a breakfast stop, came to 36:48:34. He was tired, he added in typically laconic fashion, but then he had been on his feet for a while, after all.

In 1979 Barner set a new unofficial world record after 24-hours on a California track: 162 miles, 544 yards.

In the U.S., there are no races which can compare with the Brighton and Comrades, either for longevity or as a must on the calendar. There were a good two dozen races in 1979, ranging from 50-milers in New York, California, Hawaii, Kentucky, Wyoming and Washington, including five 100-milers. One of the latter was held in Queens, N.Y., a second at Fort Meade, Maryland, and a third was the recently inaugurated Old Dominion Trail Run in Virginia, which follows very rigorous terrain in competition against horseback riders. There is also the Western States 100-Miler, which is held in Squaw Valley, California, over the High Sierra range, with 17,000 feet of total ascent. (There is some question whether the Western States is a full 100 miles.) The fifth 100-miler was held in Hawaii.

Lake Waramaug is one of the big races now, as ever-larger fields (up close to 200) opt to run the 7-plus miles around the serene waters of the Connecticut lake for 50 miles and/or 100 kilometers. Another, far better known, body of water is Lake Tahoe, which abuts onto California and Nevada and has a perimeter road of 72 miles at altitude and which attracts a small group of yearly diehards. The JFK 50-miler in Maryland is a rugged part-trail, part-road course that is taken on by a mixed bag of hikers and runners.

Every year sees new races added to the schedule, and even the fanatics have to give in to the reality that they simply can no longer run every single one. The frontiers keep expanding. After two successful 48-hour runs, Choi now has plans afoot to stage a 72-hour run in July 1980. Need more be said?

2.
In England

The London-to-Brighton run is certainly the oldest consecutive ultra race in England, but it has always had a fascination for walkers and runners. A glance at a map shows why. It goes from the heart of one of the world's great metropolises, in a satisfyingly straight southerly direction, to the nearest point on the coast. One reaches the Channel, a terminal point on the southern land tier, and looks out over the waters at the beginning of another world. It makes for a good, not-quite-too-long single trip. For the truly hardy the Brighton road makes an excellent round-trip challenge, irresistibly close to being just about 100 miles.

Therefore it comes as no surprise that one Benjamin Trench, in the year 1868, did betake himself on his two legs, walking briskly, down to Brighton and back in 23 hours. In 1897 a series of walking races was inaugurated and two running races went off about the same time. Both started at the traditional site of Big Ben—the first in 1899 and the second in 1902. Len Hurst was the 1902 winner over a 51¾-mile course in about 6½ hours. Newton, of course, chalked up an exceptional time for his era in 1924. Along the way he went through the marathon checkpoint in 2 hours and 43 minutes, which was only 90 seconds slower than the winning time that year in the Olympics!

Over the usual tea and cake, Newton talked up the idea of a regular London–Brighton running race in the postwar years when he was settled in his Ruislip Manor home. One of his listeners was Ernest Neville, a man of great energy, great enthusiasms and one of those great girths that inspires an amused confidence on the part of the beholder. Ernest Neville, in spite of the expansive white shirt front, the cigars which habitually dribbled ash over his jacket, and the thick glasses, had been an amateur athlete of a particularly keen order. He had perambulated the course 57 times, and had also founded the Centurion Club, which required any would-be member to walk 100 miles within 24 hours.

Neville was in the old line of ultra promoters—brash, energetic, stubborn and a bit of a calculating dreamer. The Festival of Britain, which was set for 1951, seemed an appropriate time to

Runners stream over Westminster Bridge at the start of the 1978 London-to-Brighton classic.

hold the first race. The bored ear of the world always takes a little convincing, and Neville and friends had difficulty in finding a sponsor for the first race. Finally the Surbiton Sports Club agreed to sponsor it. On a rain-swept day in August, 47 lined up but 32 men made it down and the race was under way as a regular business.

What was needed, clearly enough, was an organizing body that would prepare for the 1952 race, but since runners who might not want to take on such monster distances far outnumbered the others, it was soon seen as practical to expand the scope of the newly founded Road Runner's Club of England to races of 10 miles and longer. The RRC notes in its brochure, however, that it operates within the "existing strong club structure . . . the backbone of our sport." And so the dry business of organization has since provided the right setting for various hot-blooded enterprises that now form the punishingly full calendar of the English ultra scene.

Fall 1978. The morning was black and chill. Only a few cars with yellow fog lights cruised through London's ghostly streets. Down by the Thames at the foot of Westminster Bridge, hardly anyone could be seen except for a few assorted souls who stood silently about, necks pulled into windbreakers and rain ponchos, resembling a species of two-legged turtles. High overhead, the vast illuminated clockface of Big Ben thrust itself against low, swirling clouds.

When the clock hands registered three minutes before the hour of seven, a troop of runners and officials came shuttling over the bridge and took their places at the last possible instant. A London bobby, driven by the reluctant imperative of safety for the runners, strolled forward to halt motor traffic. Runners in the United Kingdom are tolerated as all the island's eccentrics are. Nonetheless, any grown man wishing to run down the main motorway to the seaside town of Brighton almost 54 miles away, who thinks he ought to take permanent precedence over the traffic as their American cousins might—well, such a delusion would be pure folly.

Needless to say, none of those gathered there expect anything better than luck and their tiny numbers as they string out along the road to shield them from the autos. English traffic is the reverse of most of the rest of the world, so the crowd of 81 on this first day of October will run on the left-hand side with their backs to the motorists. The camber, or slope, of the roadway tilts at a nasty angle, and the not infrequent storm drains are of a design just capacious enough to engulf an ill-placed foot. No matter what the trials yet to be endured on this grand morning of a grand tradition, no one must forget where feet should be placed.

British runners are not quite so flashily attired as Americans or South Africans. They are fond of wearing dark-colored socks and fairly sobersided colors for their shorts and singlets. The extra-terrestrial nylon hues of American synthetics have not reached here. The legs that belonged to this huddled tight little crew, seemed to my professional eye to be fully muscular enough, if dead white. Not much sunshine on this island. The sky had just begun to lighten into a lovely cobalt blue, which I noticed only because I glanced up at Big Ben.

"There's a pause between the introduction and the peal itself," said Bernard Gomersall, who won the race in 1964. "That pause seems so long I think it's longer than the race itself!"

I thought back to what similar mornings must have been like in 1899, or 1924, or 1931, when just one runner would stand there waiting for the signal to go, his bowler-hatted accomplices both sleepy and excited. London is not an early-rising city, especially on this Saturday morning, and there is that peculiar spirit of odd adventure abroad when one owns the almost empty streets, and the rest of the world still slumbers away unawares. Someday, I thought, others will think back to the late 1970's as a faraway time. Someone else will look at the bristle-toothed mass of the Parliament building and imagine our own contenders setting about the long run. The past always has a glamour and a heroism not often found in the present.

But such thoughts vanished as the musical peal sounded, and the familiar deep "bong" resonated through the streets. The front line set off into ragged motion. All the same, by the time I had leaped into the rented car, the anxious photographer who accompanied me leaning out of the window as we joined in pursuit, the runners were long since over the bridge and well into the serpentine roadway that leads out through London suburbs. Then we passed them on our left, already beginning to string out, setting up in twos and threes as they found their rhythm. Light began to break into a chilly white dawn as we zipped past closed shops and headed into the first symptoms of countryside. The lead runners wore tanktops, running fast, with a real stretch.

There was some shuffling around between Brixton Hill, the 3½-mile checkpoint, and the 10-mile station in outlying Croydon. Cavin Woodward—who had, as usual, snatched the lead going over the bridge—had company in the opening miles in the person of Mick Orton, former winner of Comrades and a top finisher at Brighton in recent years. The 50 yards they held over Rob Heron and Don Ritchie had evaporated by 10 miles, but their numbers were reduced to three when Orton dropped back. Shortly afterward, he was off on the side of the road, and out of the race. Woodward, Heron and Ritchie were clocked in a little under 56 minutes for ten, running at 5:35-per-mile pace.

Woodward does not like to run with others, but the other two men were clearly going to stick tight. Heron and Ritchie, the two Scots, are both red-headed and red-bearded, although there their similarities end. Ritchie is taller and runs powerfully, if not gracefully; Heron is shorter and of the trio runs the most fluidly, although he too displays the bad-mannered elbows of the rest, riding high and wide. Most ultrarunners compel admiration for their feats, but it is rare to see the sheer grace of indoor sprint men out there on the roadway. They are cutters, hackers, grinders—products of layer after layer of determination. They are together but they are concentrating on the run; they do not speak to or look at one another. The old perennial rawness of the endeavor is clear as they sweep past—to get down that road first and break the others.

These three runners all have experience, but a long day still lay ahead and they were less than twenty percent through the race. Danger men stalked them further back. Tom O'Reilly, the 1976 winner, was lying 2½ minutes behind, and Mike Newton and Tom Roden were a bit further back still. Newton and Roden had placed high before. Both were young and strong, and improving. All it takes is one breakthrough, a couple of disastrous bad patches or dropouts among the leaders, and the come-from-behind type runner could find it his day.

In spite of the danger from immediate rivals that absorbs a runner's attention, there is always the shadow stalking from behind. Falter—and others will snatch your place. The situation is always total pressure. Everyone knows that the analysis and the storytelling will go on for a year. English runners especially will be judged on their Brighton—the other races just don't matter in quite the same way. At Brighton, the time is now. The risk is now. So at 10 miles, real discomfort is yet to come and nothing is settled.

Woodward has a desire to stamp his mark on each race. At the 20-mile point he seemed to be taking over as he went through in 1:54:16, an 18-second lead over Ritchie in second, who was towing Heron another 35 seconds back. The next pair of runners were over 3 minutes behind Heron. Mathematics has its own ruthless logic. If the lead men only slow a bit—as almost everyone else will have to do as well—then the likelihood of a 5th or 6th placer making up 5 or 6 seconds per mile to close the gap to first becomes increasingly unlikely.

It does not sound like much, but to get leg speed up into a higher gear after 20 miles in the groove isn't easy. The rhythm is on, the margin of comfort is thin enough and it is hard for everyone to calculate not only how they are doing but where everyone else is as well. This is no track race, where the rivals are well in view and the clues of labored breathing or an unhappy face can spur you on. There is simply the roadway ahead. You go around the curve and look up the straight, but there is no one up ahead. The others may be about to break or they may continue to pull away.

With over 30 miles to go, the sun was making the day pleasantly warm for the spectators, who pulled off to the side of the road to shout on their boys. Refreshment stations are spaced apart, with a whimsically Spartan disregard for the lads who must look after themselves as best they can. One issue that weighs heavily on everyone's mind is not knowing how to judge the relative fitness of the others. Past performances mean little this year. How your rivals' training has gone over the past few months is probably what matters most, and few will have talked freely about that.

Shortly after 20 miles, Woodward began to accelerate and Ritchie began to lose contact.

"The start was very fast," Ritchie recalled later. "My only strategy was to hang on with the leaders. Mick Orton had trouble with his calf and dropped out. Then Rob Heron dropped off and I was just running as fast as I could, couldn't go any faster, when Cavin pulled away. I just couldn't follow and I thought, that's it."

There was a reason for that surge, which turned out to have fateful consequences on the course of the race. As usual, Carol Woodward had been driving the family car along and jumping out at regular intervals to have a word with her husband and hand him something to drink, while their three small sons gamboled by the roadside. Cavin, whose edginess about races needs soothing with such rituals as getting a haircut beforehand, learned suddenly that the car's camshaft had broken.

"I just shot ahead," he said later, "but I went off in a fog. I kept worrying how we were going to get home. I was having trouble with my right leg and my right hamstring.

"If the car hadn't broken down, I'd've run with Don a bit longer

Timers await the runners on the Brighton
road at one of the checkpoints.

and then when I'd've gone, I'd've gone for home; whereas when I
went, it was a bloody stupid time to go. There was just no way I
could hold on to it from there. Things were going well up until
then, solely because they'd dropped me for a bit there and I'd got
them back and that was encouraging. I'm with them and I'm not
feeling bad. Then the car went pssssst!"

Woodward paused in his recital and drew out the first word of
his next sentence in a long drawl. The recollection still hurt.

"Well . . . everything fell apart, didn't it?"

It wasn't apparent at all to anyone else. The first of three waves
of hills that comes between 10 and 18 miles had shaken the field
out, with about an hour separating first and last man. Woodward
was within record pace up through the top of the long hill at
Crawley. The green countryside dropped away on each side, once
one could see beyond the immediate range of trees. London was
no longer visible and the 10 a.m. traffic of beach-goers was
whizzing merrily past. A pack of cyclists in orange shirts and
black racing pants cranked up the hill, casting an indifferent look
at Woodward as, head cocked, he stormed up the long rise.
Ritchie was through shortly after, his long reaching stride still
holding steady.

"I was very surprised when Cavin started to slow down finally,"
Ritchie said. "We ran shoulder to shoulder for a while at about 34
miles, and then I pulled away, gaining about 7 seconds per mile. I
thought then I might win, because I'm quite strong over the last
part of a race."

Luck was out for Bob Heron. He had been second the year
before at Brighton, but this year just wasn't his day.

"I don't know what went wrong," Heron said later at his home
in Bognor Regis, a small seaside place not far from Brighton. "It
might have been the carbo-loading diet. I was eating lots of
raisins. I was looking for not a toilet really, just a tree or a bush. I
had to stop several times. Up over the brow of Crawley Hill
someone was waiting for me in a car. I just got in and that was
that. It took me a while to get over the disappointment."

Heron, who works as a librarian for the Institute of Higher
Education, has thought carefully about the special requirements
of ultrarunning. Shyly parting with each phrase, he spoke about
the simple rules of the game.

"You've got to be really careful about the early stages of an
ultra. You've got to be in the mood. You've got to concentrate,
but you've got to relax as much as you can. You could probably
run a marathon on a bad day and get away with it, but I don't

think there's any way you can run the Brighton on an off day. The level of fatigue is quite deep. It's inevitable because you're going longer."

The leaders approached the 40-mile point where the A23 roadway runs downward into what is half-jestingly called the Valley of Shattered Dreams. At the 42-mile point, the last great killer, Dale Hill, is yet to be gotten over. A little earlier, at a pub called Queen's Head in the township of Bolney some 39 miles from London, Ritchie was a strong first, Woodward second about a minute back, and Tom O'Reilly of Small Heath Harriers in third spot, about 7¾ minutes behind Woodward. Fourth-place man (later to finish tenth) was still back 5 minutes at that point. This meant that between the fourth and the first man was a time lag of almost 14 minutes, or a distance of over 2 miles! Shortly beyond there was the final gathering of timekeepers, officials and spectators at Pyecombe. Here Dale Hill shows its demoralizing reverse to the upward slope, a final 7-mile downhill flyaway to the sea and the finish. Ritchie barreled through without pause, having expanded his margin over Cavin by about 12 seconds in a mile in the previous 7.

Downhill running at that stage in a race will shake apart the weary, one of the reasons the Boston marathon can be a shattering experience for the weakened. Ritchie, whose string vest was already stained with blood where it had been chafing one of his nipples, gleamed with energy as he poured on the pace on the downhill into Brighton. He ran the closing stretch slightly faster than the opening of the race, at a pace just over 5:30 per mile.

The road finally flattens out with less than a mile to go, and the runners pass by the Oriental whimsy of King George IV's resort palace, the Royal Pavilion. Down at the seaside next to the blue Channel waters and the rock-strewn beachfront, the roadway makes a sharp left. At the end of a short straightaway, a signboard over the finish read "WELCOME." Two thin lines of spectators—who had stood for the past quarter hour as John Jewell gave an update on the race in crisp, measured tones over a loudspeaker—broke into dutiful applause when Ritchie rounded the corner.

Most of the people there looked like vacationers who had come along by chance. There was a bemused tolerance in their faces, as if some of them thought that adult men should be a little more sensible than to run down on foot all the way from the City.

Ritchie crossed the line, got a few handshakes, and a few words from the officials, but as he bent forward slightly, tired but smiling, a polite restraint encircled him. The crowd murmured

As Carol Woodward looks on, second-place finisher
Cavin Woodward shakes the winner's hand, 1978.

quietly to one another. Ritchie stood waiting for a good five minutes until Woodward rounded the corner and finished with a 5:18:30 time. Ritchie's own time of 5:13:02 was a new record for the new and slightly longer distance of 53 miles, 856 yards. When Woodward finished, he leaned his head on a stanchion and bent over for a moment. Then with a sigh he straightened up and shook Ritchie's hand, while his wife, holding a camera in one hand, laid her other hand lightly on his shoulder.

O'Reilly had hung on to third with a 5:38:56, over 10 minutes back from second place, and himself over 2 minutes ahead of fourth-place finisher Mike Newton. Tom Roden, Newton's colleague from the South London Harriers, was fifth. The first foreigner to finish was a Canadian in 15th place and Bill Lawder of New Jersey was the first American in 16th spot, with a 6:12 clocking which he shared with an English runner as they crossed together. Bob Myette, another American who had come over for the race, snagged 35th place with a 6:56:30. Myette was later chided for his last-minute sprint to overtake a lagging Englishman. He was told that it was not quite sporting to put on a flurry at the very finish, implying perhaps that if you run hard enough all the way through, then a last burst wouldn't be possible.

Finishers at Brighton keep their eye on their finishing time to see how they come up within the three separate time hierarchies. "First Class" times are awarded to those finishers under 6 hours and 16 minutes; "Second Class" times go to those who finish under 7 hours and 11 minutes. Half the interest of the race depends for the viewers not just on who the top men are but who their teams are. The club tradition is much stronger abroad than in the United States. In England, when runners asked me what club I was running for and I replied that I ran unattached, I got quizzical glances. "Who *would* I be running for?" they asked, certain that I had misunderstood slightly. An unattached status for a runner in England is a little akin to purgatory. Everyone belongs somewhere, and it is taken as a measure of one's seriousness and good standing in the sport, regardless of ability, to be linked with a club.

This is hardly to suggest that some mythical equivalent of the old school tie unites the warriors of each club, and that the partisanship of the soccer or rugby clubs is found on the roads. One English runner told me that "the other blokes in my club are mostly cross-country runners, and they can't be bothered about the Brighton. They don't care what you do in it. They're just thinking about their own event." All the same, scratch any ultra

man with a question about clubs, and he knows as clearly as the weather outside which teams field the strongest groups. In America, team prizes are usually not given out in ultraraces and, except for Millrose Club in New York, hardly any others think of themselves as having that specialty. In any case, the South London Harriers in 1978 were the happy possessors of the Len Hurst belt.

That award, like all the others, was given out in duly proper style only later in the afternoon, when all the runners had had a chance to bathe and change. Among the more practical traditions of the race are the warm sea-water baths, which are opened free for the runners. The changing room was a hot stench of armpits, unguents, soap and steam. The voices echoed off the old walls as, with increasing hilarity and returning vigor, the grueling episodes of the day subsided into experiences that made for a good story. A uniformed attendant, an older man, clucked over one of the runners and examined a blister on the base of his foot that was awkward to reach.

But by the time the group filtered back onto the street and wended its way four or five blocks west to the Ship Hotel, where the traditional post-race tea and award ceremony would be held, the real fatigue set in. Faces looked pale beneath the freshly wet, slicked-down hair, and the chatter was a little less animated. There was talk about getting home, and as the afternoon waned the memory of a job and other earthly concerns began to sink in a little bit. Then for a moment, when the banquet room doors swung open, there was one last bit of forgetfulness. A chance to sit down, drink tea and eat cake as Don Turner—jovial and thoroughly in command as president of the Road Runner's Club—presented the various awards and offered kind words to the foreigners, mostly American, who were present.

The English officials were all in suit and tie, a kind of well-bred counterpart to the so recently skimpily attired men they shepherded down from Brighton. The Lord Mayor of Brighton, resplendent in the gold chains of his office, issued forth with various words about the whole business. He was blessed in return by three rounds of "Hip-hip-hooray," from the assembled guests. I felt sorry for him, having to dream up something to say about these lunatics who happened to have picked his constituency as a place to run down to every year. But they were duly welcomed and even encouraged to return the following year.

The applause had petered off, as it must, by the time the finishers in 40th place and beyond went up for their handshake and a certificate, with a red route line squiggling from top to

It feels good to sit down after covering 53½ miles from London.

bottom. As such things go, it is a classy-looking document. Next, like schoolboys receiving examination papers, we passed from one end of the long dining tables to the other for mimeographed copies of the results. The efficiency of the tabulators was remarkable, and as a veteran of innumerable road races where award ceremonies dawdle on into the eleventh hour of the day, it was a relief to be part of such a briskly handled operation.

Suddenly it was over. The hall rustled briefly during the exodus. The final word, as always, would appear in a later issue of the Road Runner's Club's *Newsletter*, one of those classic little magazines with a tiny circulation, whose race accounts are gems of their kind. A pamphlet-sized publication that features a few telling black and white photographs, each important marathon and ultrarace of the season gets a detailed rundown within. The race is told as a story with a beginning, a middle and an end, with splits and running paces included. Temperature, wind, type of course—all the nitty-gritty detail that make up the classic simplicity of a runner's world, are laid down in simple prose. The precision and the care of the English, which can sometimes seem to an American a little too fine and fussy, are at their best here, where the passion for the sport can be seen as something pure, shorn of overt histrionics and ego trumpetings.

Over the years, different Americans have run the Brighton course and a handful have done extremely well. Ted Corbitt of New York wore the New York Pioneer Club shirt 5 times down the Brighton road, and took second three times. One issue of the RRC *Newsletter* commented that he was one of the "unluckiest" competitors in the race "never to have been the winner." Corbitt was one of the very few Americans to go over to England to run Brighton in the 1960's and, until a few years ago, the only one who tried his hand at some of the track 100-mile and 24-hour races.

Max White, now a Virginia schoolteacher, was a graduate-school student in 1973 when, at the age of 22, he logged an outstanding 5:26:26 over a then 52½-mile course. He took fourth in the race, which still stands as the fastest American time. In 1977 the New York Millrose Club was led by ex-fireman Gary Muhrcke, himself third in the race as he anchored his team to the only first-place finish an American team has yet netted.

In 1979 Allan Kirik of the Central Park Track Club became the first American to win the race—over a new 54 mile, 460 yard distance—with a 5:32:37 clocking.

The real foreign competition, however, has always come from

South Africa. The connections are obvious and deep. A number of English runners have gone down there to work, and sometimes to settle permanently. Other Englishmen went down to run the Comrades and settle a few scores of their own in the only other ultra they considered traveling any distance for. The friendships, the rivalries and the connections were deeply intertwined.

All this is now in the past, however, for in 1976 a ban imposed by the IAAF made it impossible for amateur athletes from any other country to compete in international races in South Africa. Similarly, South African runners cannot go abroad to compete officially. The old link dating back to the days of Arthur Newton, Ballington, Hayward, Mekler and Morrison, on up through the likes of Dave Bagshaw, a Yorkshireman who copped the Comrades first place three times, has gone into suspension.

There is a quiet disgruntlement on the part of English runners at being deprived of the chance to ever get down to run Comrades. They are not unsympathetic to the political and racial questions raised about South Africa but, like South African runners themselves, they are skeptical about the relationship between running and politics. They simply want to run, and if the race is now open to all racial groups they feel, naturally enough, that they themselves have little to do with the bigger questions. They are sportsmen and impatient of anything that interferes with that. But conversations on this subject end with a shrug and the comment that the rules are the rules, aren't they?—too bad, but nothing can be done. The new restrictions have a far greater effect on South Africans themselves, who can now only run within their own country. For the English it means only the loss of a single great race.

3.
In South Africa

There is one question that every non–South African wants answered. I knew I would have to ask this question when I went there and I did. The South African runners to whom I put it showed not the slightest surprise when I brought up the problem of racial equality, not only in sports but in society at large. For whether or not you believe that politics and sports should be joined together, they frequently are.

I spent three weeks in South Africa, forming impressions that were somewhat more complex than I had expected they would be.

Much to my surprise and pleasure, I found that road running and track, probably more than any other sports in South Africa, have opened up, to a very considerable degree, to the admission of non-whites on an equal basis. For runners, the major area of inequality left is the matter of integrating club bars. The club structure in South Africa is very dominant in amateur athletics. And since having a pint or two after a weekly club race, or on a weekend, is as much a part of the attraction for the convivial South African spirit as the actual run, it is clearly an absurdity to bar fellow teammates and competitors from entering the tap rooms when the showers, lockers and running tracks are open to them.

Every white South African runner I spoke to was unhappy over the fact, but clubs are not permitted to violate national legislation which prohibits whites and non-whites from drinking together in private clubs. Although most outsiders view apartheid, the legal framework which fosters the separation of races in South Africa, as aimed at blacks, it actually applies to any non-white identified as being African, colored or Indian. South Africa has four million whites and twenty million non-whites. Everyone agrees that the status quo will not last. Whether or not the slow changes occurring are taking place fast enough or extensively enough is obviously a matter of opinion, depending on which side of the color barrier you view the matter from.

In 1975, just a few years ago, Comrades became officially integrated. Previously, non-white competitors had run without numbers. Encouraged and cheered on like everyone else, they were nonetheless unofficial, second-class citizens. That was also the year women were allowed as official entrants in Comrades—over the protests of many running-circle officials—and since then, change has come quickly. In 1976, prohibitions against clubs admitting non-whites were eased so that blacks could join, although at this writing eating and drinking facilities remain closed to non-whites.

The Springbok national colors have now been awarded to outstanding black runners. On a national prime-time TV show in May of 1979, I watched a black runner whose nickname in Afrikaans means literally "Running Fall" (because of his idiosyncratic way of jutting his neck and shoulders forward) surge to the front of the pack in a 10,000-meter race and hold the competition at bay. He is a respected national figure among sports enthusiasts. On a personal level, interaction between whites, black Africans and Asians at Comrades was, as far as I could sense, totally unself-conscious. There were no questions about sharing water bottles during the run, or a hug and a handshake on the other side of the finish line. Before a 5-mile club-time trial in Johannesburg, there was some easy joshing between a couple of black runners who belong to the club and their club brothers. But as the pace crackled along after the start, and one of the African runners and I stuck it out for 3 miles through the gloom of an early dusk up and down over the hills, there was no easy exchange of liberal clichés. We were both runners and we went at it until, wheezing from the altitude, I had to let him get away. But many gaps still remain. Those same two joshing runners had to ask around to get a lift back to their segregated township, since they didn't own a car, as most white runners do.

I heard one story about the finish of a long-distance road race, when the African who unexpectedly won seemed nervous and apprehensive, almost embarrassed, at what might have been his effrontery in taking first. But he realized quickly enough that the yelling was *for* him, not at him. Still, this is a telling anecdote. The number of non-white ultrarunners is relatively quite small still. Vincent Rakabeale, who works for one of the mining companies, is the runner best known in ultra circles for his tenacious trailing of the leaders—and some occasional wins, including a recent 2:20:08 marathon at altitude.

The best-known black runner from South Africa in the outside world is Sydney Maree, an undergraduate whose tremendous talent on the track has won him the green and gold Springbok shirt. Maree, now 22, ran a 3:57:9 schoolboy mile, second fastest

The annual Comrades 54-miler has been integrated since 1975.

on record. Early in 1979, on an outdoor track in South Africa with Prime Minister John Voerster watching in the stands, Maree ran a 3:53:7 mile, a new South African record. Not only is Maree a world-class miler, he's also a strong 5,000-meter contender. But he is unable to compete in international meets—as all South Africans, regardless of color, have been since 1970. That year the International Amateur Athletic Federation (IAAF) voted to ban South Africa from all international team competition in track and field.

Individual athletes came under the ban in 1976. Under this ruling no runners from abroad can compete in South Africa. Those who violate this rule can lose their amateur status and be barred from the Olympics, as South Africa is at present. Although other white runners from various countries are willing to run against Maree, the threat of sanctions means that Maree must sit out important meets in the stands. Thus the toughest competition he can face is denied to him while he's in his prime. In a sense this prohibition, designed to put political pressure on the white government to change its policies toward non-whites, holds back athletes of all races, which strikes me as a very sad situation. There are counter arguments—to wit, that without the continual pressure of a ban, change will not continue and the success of a few outstanding black runners will "paint an inaccurate picture of the hardships faced by South African blacks." It's not a very simple situation or one likely to be quickly resolved.

For South Africans, the annual Comrades Marathon is a fever, a passion, a rally against the slothfulness of civilization that shakes you till your teeth rattle. But all who finish are redeemed by being made men—and nowadays, women. It's a grand old democratic hubbub with entrants ranging from the minimally talented to ultrarunners who could hold their own with the best in the world. Comrades is the only road race that matters to road runners—not just the distance specialists but any runner who steps off the track. The Washie 100-miler that is run on the southern coast under the light of the full moon, the Korkie 36-miler, any of the standard marathons—whatever other races the calendar offers are pale moons far outshone by Comrades.

On race day every year at the end of May, helicopters chug overhead, a staff car from Radio Port Natal hugs the heels of the lead runners, and an excited live commentary is beamed out around the province while the rest of the nation gets phoned-in, on-the-spot reports every hour. The papers splash the results on their front pages, chronicling the several-day buildup in multicolored inks detailing the course and the rules, remembering the old heroes, rehashing in an unabashedly barrelful-of-clichés kind of way how the Comrades race is "the greatest in the world," a saga of struggle against misfortune and pain. The greater the drama, the more the sports-minded public loves it.

The greatest honor for an athlete here is to be awarded either a Springbok shirt with the national colors—given to athletes who represent South Africa in international amateur competition—or to win Comrades. Win it several times and your name will always be remembered. Countrymen will be fond of you, immortalize your name in little booklets about the race, seek you out when you're really fit for nothing more strenuous than a stroll around town in colonial Bermudas with knee socks, to solicit your recollection of the old days and your assessment of the present generation of speedsters.

All the same, the largesse of South Africa's adoration is extended not just to Wally Hayward, or Jackie Mekler, or Alan Robb, but to the great characters who have pranced over the 53- or 54-mile-long course—depending on the year—and acquitted themselves with style. People talk about Robin Stamper, the South African Airways pilot, who's been known to dash off ahead of the field only to be passed later on by the other runners while he lies by the side of the road, his feet perched up against a tree, only to jump in later and still finish high up.

They talk about Cecil (Bill) Payn, a rugby Springbok and a friend of Arthur Newton's who ran the second race in 1922. Payn, a schoolteacher, ran the race as a lark. He picked up a whopping thirst from the dusty roads—to say nothing of a healthy appetite, and he stopped along the way to consume 39 oranges, 3 gallons of various liquids and a lunch of steak and chips. At Hill Crest he also ate a "huge plate of bacon and eggs" topped off by curried chicken "in a snowdrift of rice." Payn, in a supremely casual gesture, was in his rugby boots and treated his blistered feet with Brilliantine. At some point later in the race, he was persuaded with a little difficulty by one of the officials to leave his glass of beer at the pub and get on with it. All the same, Payn was not to be denied further refreshments. At Harrison Flats, he later recalled: "I noticed a frail little woman with pink cheeks standing at the side of the road. She held up in one hand a bottle, and in the other a glass. I stopped and with old-world courtesy bowed low, saying: 'Madame, your servant to command.' 'It's peach brandy,' she volunteered, 'and I make it myself.'" It was potent stuff, apparently, but it served to propel Payn on toward Maritzburg, where the race finished that year. He made a final stop for a spot of tea and cake with his in-laws. All the same, Payn finished eighth with a time of 10 hours and 56 minutes, still within the cut-off point of the modern-day race. The following day he played in a rugby match.

There is a universal pride among the players in the Comrades drama about the back three-quarters of the field. In 1979, at the club quarters of the Collegians Harriers, organizers of the Comrades race, I was introduced over a pint of bitters to a portly gentleman with a full, curly salt-and-pepper beard. Yes, he said, it was true that he was training again for Comrades—in spite of having had most of his stomach removed because of cancer. He lifted his blue warm-up top and displayed a swath of hairy belly, disfigured by a tremendous sear of white scar tissue. Qualifying times are generally stretched to include anyone with a reasonable hope of finishing before the 11-hour cut-off point, and for quite a number of entrants it is a training job of 4 or 5 months only that they rely on to get them through.

"Comrades is a completely different kettle of fish than the Brighton," asserted Mick Winn, the tall, well-dressed chief organizer of the race. A pharmacist in Pietermaritzburg, Winn has a lean, military look about him. His stern face lifts occasionally in a smile as he talks, but it is apparent that all his drive and passion, now that he no longer runs the race himself, is dedicated to making its demanding logistics come off as well as possible.

"The main goal of the individual here," Winn said, "is simply to finish the race—even among some of the top runners. It is one of the few races that presents a challenge to everyone. In a way it's a glorified fun run. All shapes and sizes meet it and beat it. It's not only for the great athletes. Sixty percent of the field finishes 7 hours after the race starts, and twenty percent of the field gets in in the last hour! But once you do the 'up' course one year, then of course you must try the 'down' course the other. Or vice versa. And then you want to improve your time, so there you are suddenly hooked on the race forever."

As soon as the computerized results of the 1979 Comrades Marathon were ready, typesetters at *The Natal Witness* went to work on the following day's edition. On page 16, deep in one of the dense columns of agate type, was buried the following cryptic announcement: "559 Sherrard, A., 7.58." Not many breakfast slurpers of tea would have paused long enough to read through the 558 names that preceded the name of Tony Sherrard— a Johannesburg executive, married, stepfather of two boys, competitor in his ninth consecutive Comrades at the age of 34. Nor, if they reached his name, would they be likely to recognize it as belonging to one of the more dedicated members of the Rand Athletic Club and one of the regular competitors in the club's Wednesday night run. This run pelts through darkened suburban streets, over back lawns, up hills and down dales before returning 5 miles later in the thin air high above sea level to the starting point. That thin line of newspaper type was at once a credit to Sherrard's persistence and a reminder of a man nursing not only tired legs but mixed feelings. This was the year he wanted to break 7½ hours and at last get a silver medal, but it had not been a good day. So Tony would have to be satisfied with the 7-hours-58-minutes clocking, and with the ninth strip badge he could now have his wife, Janet, sew onto an athletic warmup jacket that bristles with multifarious legends and cloth labels testifying to various outlandish ultra enterprises.

"The white South African has a very sophisticated, civilized standard of living," Sherrard told me, in an attempt to explain why he ran the Comrades. "But he has no more targets. The whole world's been explored, and all the things his ancestors had to struggle with are gone, so he has to find feats of endurance. The average man has found when attempting Comrades that it's an outstanding achievement to make it through. I feel this way myself.

"I used to lead a pretty plastic life, staying out in discos until four in the morning, but it doesn't get you anywhere. Running has changed my life. I enjoy my life now. The running calendar in South Africa is based on Comrades. From June to June. That's one of the reasons we haven't done so well as a country in the standard marathons—everyone aims for the glory of the Comrades. The mileage you need for it slows you down.

"Brighton used to be the event to go to after Comrades, but because of the sports ban it has lost its appeal. It hurts not to run there in a way, but I think the guys worry more now when they can't do it than when they could do it. As it is most guys go into hibernation after Comrades, and there is a noticeable decline in performance and times. There are some more ultraraces coming along, like the Washie 100-miler and the Joburg to Pretoria 50-kilometer race to keep a better standard up."

Comrades is run in alternate years from the town hall in Durban and the town hall in Pietermaritzburg, as the chimes of the clocks sound six a.m. Since the province of Natal in which the race is run abuts on the Indian Ocean, even in winter the area is subject to a

Two South African ultrarunners finish
in the Comrades spirit.

tropical heat. When the race leaves Durban, which is at sea level, the difficulties of the "up" course seem overwhelming. Within 12 miles the runners must climb over 1,300 feet and then, in the next two miles, climb another 500 feet. Umlaas Road, the highest point on the course, tops off at 2,606 feet above sea level, and from there on in to the finish it is generally a fastish downhill. Such statistics are hard to inject with much substance. Only by driving or running over it do the steep grinds uphill seem as shockingly bad as they really are. The so-called "down" course inevitably includes a good deal of hill climbing as well, and the closing 20 miles down to the Indian Ocean wreak severe punishment on all but the strongest. Running downhill is no treat at the end of an ultrarace, since only the fastest runners can lean into the downhill pitch and avoid the otherwise inevitable tendency to brake with the full force of their body weight.

Over the years the course has changed in character with the installation of a new freeway parallel to the old road. The present course is a bewildering in-and-out splicework of both roadways but the basic rise and fall through the valleys and countryside is about the same as it once was, although of course the roadway has improved considerably since 1921, the year of the first race. The first man who actually ran the road on a regular basis was an African of the Zulu tribe whose name has now been forgotten. In the spring of 1846, he was hired by the editor of a new weekly newspaper in Pietermaritzburg to carry a package of the papers down to Durban for distribution. He regularly "took about 12 hours, rain or shine, to do the journey, and was very proud of his punctuality."

On May 31, 1979, on a South African national holiday called Empire Day, a light went on in the house of Adrian Alexander. Known familiarly as "Bullet" because of the shape of his head, he is one of the prime movers in organizing Comrades. It was not yet three a.m. but it was race day and Bullet had work to do, putting up signboards along the course that would announce every 5 kilometers what distance was left to complete the 88.2-kilometer course. It had already taken 14 hours to measure the route with a measuring wheel one foot away from the edge of the curb.

Bullet, whose genial ways belie the nickname, is a veritable fountain of facts and figures about the problems of thirst and appetite the runners will encounter. He is well imbued with the Comrades spirit and is a veteran of the race. He started running at 32 when an old friend died of thrombosis, a tragedy which frightened him into concern about his own fitness. Bullet is a believer in the magic of the race and says: "I honestly feel that Comrades is the reason ultrarunning is so popular in South Africa." Certainly Comrades sets a standard for organization few ultraraces can match.

Some 1,200 people are involved this May morning to make sure that all goes well. They are all needed. This year about 3,400 applications were mailed in; approximately 3,000 persons are expected to begin registration at the Durban Town Hall at five a.m. Forty-seven refreshment stations are spaced out along the route to prevent the perennial dozen or so runners who are shuttled off to hospitals with dehydration or heat stroke. Ten sponging stations are manned by bevies of attractive women. In all 24,380 liters of Coke, 30,000 liters of water, 114,000 plastic drink bottles and 28,000 sponges—not to mention an indeterminate amount of Vaseline—will be provided. The entry fee of a little over two dollars entitles each finisher to either a gold, silver or bronze medal (depending on the finishing time), a Comrades badge, a Comrades tape, both of which can be sewn onto their running jackets, plus any refreshments and medical care required. Between the money from the entry fees and a limited amount of commercial sponsorship, which is carefully screened, the Comrades committee manages every year to break even on expenses.

One problem with the phenomenal increase in the size of the field (up five times from what it was 10 years ago) is the increased motor traffic along the route. Ever stricter controls have cut back into the time-honored practice of having handlers drive or ride alongside their runners with advice and special foods and drinks—a practice leading in modern times to horrendous traffic jams and clouds of blue exhaust fumes for the already embattled participants. More responsibility is placed on the organizers who, as it is, start planning a year in advance of each race. All the same it is now typical for over 95 percent of the starters to finish the race, a very high figure even when compared to much smaller races.

There are usually enough runners either in one's club or one's neighborhood to make training a lot easier. The Germiston Callies Club of Johannesburg, which boasts about a thousand members, is devoted to track, cross-country and road racing. About 500 members are road runners. Of that number about 250 run Comrades. On a club run in the final weeks leading to Comrades, as many as a hundred runners might go out for a group training run.

Sherrard will take to the road on Sundays himself with some of his own RAC teammates. A sleepy-eyed group meets at Len

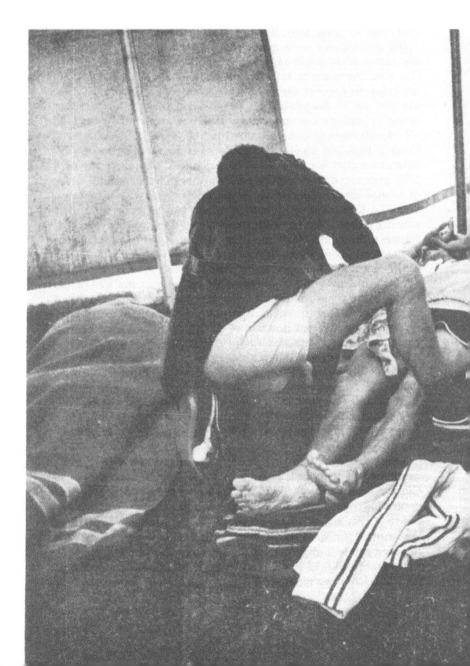

Exhausted South African athletes get help in the first-aid tent after running 54 hilly miles.

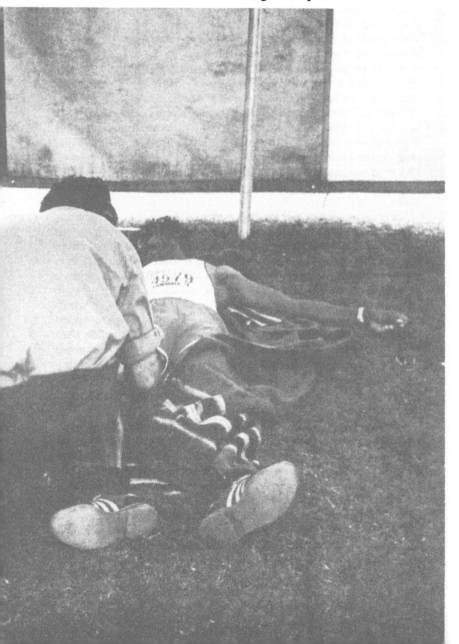

Keating's house at seven in the morning, while the shadows are still thick on the ground. Keating, a tall, rangy-looking man with short-cropped grayish hair, speaks softly but with the glowing fanaticism of an ultrarunner whose training is going well, and who is illuminated from deep within by present ambitions. Like Sherrard, and the other South Africans I have met who chronicle for me their "new lives," the displaced intensity with which these men once pursued the good life is now just as strongly at work in hammering their bodies into road fitness.

As we strike out along the already shimmering roadways that the hot May sunshine of early morning is turning uncomfortably toasty, we occasionally pass African workers. Keating greets some of them in Zulu or Shona or other local dialects and they call back in reply, a little surprised by the white man's fluent greeting. Keating, who formerly lived in Rhodesia where he was manager of a department store, said that he "just gradually faded away, like most people. Rhodesia is a very relaxed and easygoing life. I was smoking three packs a day and putting away ten or twelve beers a night."

Twelve years earlier he had suffered from the excruciating agony of a collapsed lung, which brought him gasping to his knees. On his 35th birthday he resolved to start running. From the quarter mile he attempted the first time, which left him retching by the roadside, he moved on to lose 50 pounds within a year. He now weighs about 160 pounds and stands 6' 2". He began running his first ultras in Rhodesia, including a 33-miler which went along a route so threatened by terrorists that he was seconded by his Rhodesian Army mates off the back of a truck, while they held their rifles at the ready. In more relaxed circumstances Keating set up a new Rhodesian record for 24 hours on a hot day on a hard-baked track with 134 miles, 389 yards. Now living in Johannesburg with his wife and sons, he is another confirmed Comrades bug.

Comrades still begins at the traditional hour, but the smooth asphalt highway is vastly different than it was when Vernon Jones watched the first race begin in 1921, with a tiny parade of about 20 grimy runners, a few motorcars and some pedal bikes.

"I was 12 years old in 1921," Jones told me, "and I was at a scout camp at Pinetown, which is about 7 miles from Durban. You could barely call it a hamlet then, it was such a tiny place. We heard about this fabulous thing where these men were going to try to run to Maritzburg. We couldn't believe it. We were most impressed. Of course then the road was dusty, and little of it was

Sometimes exhaustion hits the hardest the
moment the struggle to the finish ends.

tarred. It was rough. Oh, grim! It was just after the Great War
and only the privileged few had motor cars. If you didn't take the
daily train service, you had to get along on a push-bike and, well,
you were lucky if you got through with less than half a dozen
punctures from sharp stones. It was such a lonely road. Even in
my day a bit later, it was so undeveloped you could go 10 miles
without seeing a building. There was no water around. We used
to stick 25 to 50 cents—which was a lot of money then—in our
pockets and just set off for the other end. If there was no tea room
for the next 10 miles, then we'd just have to go without a drink.
Today your pampered third-rater wants first-class attention every
100 yards or so, which is humbug really. Anyway, this first race I
saw was a complete rookie thing for the runners and the organizer. Clapham was not in any way an athlete himself. He had this
idea of his, and he was called an idiot for suggesting that chaps
could run it."

My chauffeur and guide on race day is Mike Toms, an old
hand at the South African Broadcasting System, who is covering
the race today as part of his sports beat. Toms gives his son a few
details to jot down and slides in behind the wheel. With a debo-
nair but hair-raising insouciance, Toms retells in effortless form
various anecdotes about the races in years past, while surging
ahead of slower vehicles and runners until we're up near the front
of the race. Short and dapper, his clothes carefully groomed and
his mustache finely clipped, Toms has a mission: to broadcast live
a phoned-in report over the SABS for all of Africa during the race
every hour, and then to broadcast a wrap-up from the finish in
Maritzburg. He is infinitely polite to me, but all steel when stolid
traffic policemen or occasional knots of cars clog our way.

"This is the worst day of the year for me," Toms says, "I hardly
sleep at all. The race has gotten bigger each year, because the
jogging boom here has led naturally to a lot of interest in Comrades. People are worried about their health, too. South Africa
has the highest incidence of heart attacks among whites in the
world. Comrades is the greatest sporting event in the country.
Nothing sparks my admiration quite the way this does.

"I can remember the greatest moment that ever happened in a
Comrades, and it's one that epitomizes the whole thing to me. In
1967, Tommy Malone, a little Englishman, had led virtually from
start to finish on a down run. At Pinetown, with about 22 kilometers to go, he was at least 3 minutes ahead of Manie Kuhn, a man
who'd done quite well in previous years. We were standing at the
finish listening to the walkie-talkie system. Tommy Malone had

gotten ill and Kuhn was catching up, but we were pretty confident that Malone was going to win. When the system broke down, no further news came in. Finally at the appointed time, at 5 hours and 50 minutes, we got word that the leading runner was nearing the stadium. As the commentator, I was looking up the finishing straight but couldn't see further than 100 meters. Back at the radio station, the announcer said: 'For news of the 1967 Comrades Marathon we switch over . . .' And I went on saying, 'Yes, and there he comes. Tommy Malone seems to come out of the crowd carrying in his hand the cylinder which he just was handed, containing the goodwill message from the mayor of Martizburg to the mayor of Durban. Here he comes, the winner of . . .' And all of a sudden there was a shout from the crowd and Manie Kuhn came through, going like a steam engine. Malone heard the crowd. He tried to sprint, fell with the cylinder still in his hand. Twenty meters from the tape he fell again. Two meters from the tape down again. Manie Kuhn said later: 'I nearly let him win the race and then I thought, I couldn't—the hell with it.' And he just passed Malone, who had his arms outstretched toward the finish line. It was the greatest finish we can ever hope to see. The difference in their times was one second. The bedlam was unbelievable.

"I was still new to the game. I had always vowed to myself I would remain in control. I heard the tapes later. I'd screamed into the mike, distortion all over the place. And the other memory I always carry of the race is to see the official stand at the finish line with his back to the straight, looking at his watch and firing the gun at exactly 11 hours after the start. It is heartbreaking to see men who run in, who will get no official recognition."

Another footnote to that race came from Vernon Jones, a longtime participant and supporter of Comrades, who said: "Malone always contended that it wasn't leg cramp that did him in but a kind of paralysis of his thigh muscles. It was an occupational hazard, due to the gases from some kind of electronics he was working with. After a long bout of trouble with his Achilles tendons, he found they were doing the work of the wasted thigh muscles. Even now he does his first 5 miles or so just limping until he warms up. He was going to run this year but his tendons broke down again."

At 5:45 the broad avenue in front of Durban City Hall is filled with the usual mob of runners so familiar to the start of large marathons in New York City or Boston or anywhere. It is a little awesome to realize how far they will be running. The usual gay pre-race pandemonium prevailed. Palm trees rustle in the mild pre-dawn breeze, and birds chatter angrily. The sturdy-legged troops of tanned men and women who have invaded this easygoing resort center in the past few days are all together at last. Max Trimborn, well into his late 70's, is called upon to signal the race with his imitation of a cock's call as the town hall clock sounds six.

Up the road on the edge of town, the first climb looms as a swift reminder that the race is on. The flashing blue lights of the police car, cruising along just in front of the leaders, forms bright halos in the light mist. Two lines of people already crowd each side of the street, and at the bridge overpass on the highway a crowd of sleepy children and parents fill it to capacity. A familiar ritual for families who live along the early stages of the route is to sit in front of their homes in pajamas and bathrobes, watching the throng go past before retiring indoors for breakfast. As a couple of runners storm past in the lead, with a trailing pack of some 15 men 20 seconds behind them, the old special thrill of the race renews itself, although it is strange to be on the outside looking on. The running looks effortless and quiet.

Everyone's interest centers around the two runners likeliest to win. There is the hard-slogging, slow-starting Alan Robb, the 25-year-old who has already won Comrades 3 times in a row. Although reticent around the press, he is candid enough to say that he wants 5 wins in a row. He doesn't care for the pressure, he says, of being considered so superhuman that he is not subject to cramps or a rotten day like anyone else. His paper matchup is 29-year-old Johnny Halberstadt, one of South Africa's best marathoners with a very fast 2:15:08 to his credit. His marathon credentials certainly make his legs a pair of the very fastest to ever step up to the ultra distances, and the question is whether his lack of experience—this is his first ultra race—will mean too fast a start and a consequent later burnout. Cheerfully granting interviews while demonstrating his specially designed shoes, Halberstadt is realistic about the difficulty of winning but makes a point of saying that his strategy, based on a study of every winner since 1964, is well laid out.

There are other danger men as well, and "Waltzing Dave" Wright is among them. Wright, who has run Comrades 6 times previously, has a habit of finishing his races—as in 1978 when he took second place—with arms outspread and his tired feet doing a bit of a waltzing shuffle, much to the delight of the grandstand. Wright could be there along with a few others, if anyone else at the lead falters, but the real dark horse of the race will turn out to be someone no one really guessed at. For the moment it is Halberstadt who dominates the race, as his small frame—with the long reaching stride of a track runner—clips through the opening miles with a steady, relaxed style, elbows slightly akimbo, his bearded face set and serious as he plows along. He looks neither to the right nor the left from under his visored cap, his longish hair on the nape of his neck flapping with each step's impact.

The forecast is for cloudy, overcast weather but soon the morning chill is gone, and the weather turns warmish and close. At Westville, about 7 miles into the race, Halberstadt is building a comfortable margin of almost 50 seconds on Steve Atkins of the Durban Athletic Club, a muscular-looking runner whose strong bearded face remains impassive. Alan Robb is back about another 30 seconds in with a small pack that includes Waltzing Dave.

Halberstadt cruises through Pinetown 5 kilometers later with another 40 seconds added to his previous margin. As the slight figure in red shorts, white vest and yellow cap runs on alone, the chopper overhead yammers excitedly, and on the road itself a few motorbikes and cars dog the man who is clearly becoming the race's favorite. Positions behind him remain relatively unchanged.

Ten more kilometers slip by and the Johannesburg Wanderers runner in the front of the race begins to "O" with his mouth as he breathes, the first real sign of strain he shows as he forces the pace alone. Six more kilometers are passed as the inland skies cloud and the day suddenly turns cooler. Halberstadt seems back in control, his reddish beard almost glowing with heat as he opens up over 2 minutes between him and Piet Vorster, another bearded runner. Vorster, who matched strides earlier with his look-alike, Atkins, has shaken free, leaving Atkins holding 3rd while a pale Wright and a haggard-looking Robb are in with the trailing lead packs.

The steep winding climb up Botha's Hill is where the country-side begins to unroll in one green-misted curl of land after another, in the region known as Valley of a Thousand Hills. The road goes past Africans, many of them Zulus, the children bare-foot and in shorts, waiting to see the runners pass—especially the black ones—giving ululating cries of encouragement. Past a boy's school with all the young men turned out in khaki shorts, knee socks, sweaters, all looking trim with pink English faces.

At Drummond, the halfway point, there is a hotel just down the road where a number of cars and officials have gathered to see the first runners through. Sure enough, it is still Halberstadt with

An African runner gets some encouragement
near the end of the 1979 Comrades race.

a 26-odd-mile time of 2:45:30, which may sound a little slow to anyone who hasn't seen the course, but is inside the previous "up" time by a startling 4½ minutes. Halberstadt has been averaging 6:07 minutes per mile, and if he continues to maintain that pace will take a good 15–20 minutes off the up record. Four minutes later, a strong and confident Piet Vorster runs through. He almost didn't make it that morning to the check-in, a bad ankle having convinced him that he shouldn't even try the run. Only the arguments of his brother and his second convinced him to do it, but the prolonged discussion delayed his check-in to just moments before the starting gun. Not until halfway did Vorster think he might go the whole way.

For Alan Robb, it is simply a bad run from the beginning. A week before the race, he came down with flu, and his legs never got over feeling leaden. It isn't apparent till the halfway point how bad he is really feeling. Robb characterizes his running style as "a sort of shuffle." He appears to run four strides to every three of his competitors, and watching him it is hard to imagine the closing determination and speed he had mustered in the previous three Comrades. As he begins to bump down toward 12th place, it seems clear that only a late miracle can get him to the line ahead of Halberstadt.

But the lead runner's fortunes are beginning to shift, as so often happens in the second half of the race. It isn't easy to lead the whole way. With 32 kilometers left to go, Halberstadt seems in some subtle way to show the touch-and-go quality he is struggling with. On an upslope before the Nagle Dam turnoff, he isn't running with the same deep determination as before. A while later, going through Cato Ridge, his muscles quiver with each stride as he runs and his entire body color changes hue. The gap between him and Vorster narrows slightly as the second man, bright-looking, eyes aware from under his dark eyebrows, continues to move strongly. Dave Wright has taken third slot.

Two days before, sitting with his girlfriend at an outdoor table sipping a soft drink, Wright speculated on what he might be feeling at this point.

"Everyone experiences fatigue," Wright said. "It's like a friend at the end of the race, and it won't get too much worse. It's just after halfway that the freshness evaporates. It's almost a booby prize to be leading at the halfway point. It's a barren stretch—those closing miles, running through that dry countryside—if you're not in front and not in a pack either, because the field is spread out by that point. You wonder, why am I running this? It can seem totally meaningless if you're in agony. It's gruelingly lonely being out there on your own. I try to concentrate on my position, realistic things, tell myself you can keep this pace up, don't worry. For most people this is do-or-die, but I have a cavalier attitude about running. You know, it's not my whole life. Certainly I'd like to win, the same as anyone else, and I'll try for it."

By the time we have stationed ourselves along the highway near Mpsuleni, 13 kilometers or so from the finish, dramatic news has already broken on the radio. A weeping announcer has declared that Johnny Halberstadt is "down on the ground, off to the side, ladies and gentlemen, apparently getting a massage. This courageous running, which . . ." and so on and so on. The fortunes of the race have shifted at last for Piet Vorster and he has nipped by a walking Halberstadt to take command of the race, with no one else near enough to mount a challenge. Now the tag-along motorbikes, who have picked the wrong man to follow, attach themselves to the new leader, like sucker fish moving to a more likely prize.

Vorster, whom hardly anyone had picked beforehand as a likely winner, never falters as he runs down through the last stretch to Jan Smuts Stadium, where a crowd of several thousand including his very pregnant wife await his arrival. He grins through his beard at everyone, after giving his wife a hug and a kiss, his long black hair plastered down with sweat.

He is a hero. He has set a new course record of 5:45:02, more than two minutes under the old record. Five minutes and 28 seconds later, Halberstadt runs in, doing the final lap on the grass in front of the crowd before making the last turn into the short straightaway. Third man in is a university student, Bruce Fordyce, with a 5:51:15; fourth man comes in about 9 minutes later and then a very disappointed-looking Alan Robb is fifth in 6:01:12. There is a great cheer for him, but after putting his hand to his face for an instant he walks grimly away. No one trails after him or dares to say a word. Dave Wright goes into his dance step shortly before doing a cartwheel over the line in 10th place with a 6:04:58. He smiles but his face is waxen and strained.

Lettie Van Zyl, who at the age of 45 insists she doesn't feel old—certainly not too old to be winning Comrades, is resigned at not taking first place for the same Comrades Bowl award that went to her in 1977 and 1978, as the first lady finisher. Mrs. Van Zyl says some people call her a tractor because "Once I'm chugging, I'm chugging!"

"Now that some of the other girls have beaten me, I take my

Johnny Halberstadt, second in the 1979 Comrades,
talks to the press, while Piet Vorster, the winner, listens.

After two consecutive wins a disappointed Alan Robb
fails to win Comrades a third year in a row.

hat off to them," Mrs. Van Zyl later said with a laugh. She has broad, strong features, wears glasses and has short black hair. She looks like a no-nonsense person.

"I know the younger girls are getting stronger and better. There were just a few of us unofficially when I ran my first Comrades back in 1973. Then the bug hit me.

"Actually it was my husband Phillip who started me. We had been married eleven years then and he told me I should run, too, because it was good for my health. I was 29 and all I could do was get around the block once. I tried cross-country and later race walking, where I once did 7 hours and 35 minutes for 37 miles. Phillip said if you can do that you can do Comrades. I said to him, 'You must be mad.' The first year I did a 9:08 on the down course."

Since 1973 Mrs. Van Zyl has improved her down time to an 8:25 and her up time to an 8:32.

Gold medals went to the top ten finishers. Silver medals went to those who finished under 7½ hours (337 runners) and bronze medallions were the rewards of those who finished before the 11-hour cut-off (2,574 runners). Of the close to 3,000 runners who started, the vast majority (2,811 all told) finished within the time limit. There were a few others who came in, and even for them the crowd stayed on.

Mick Winn stepped up to the finish line with about a minute to go. He had already had an emotional day. When his 18-year-old son, Graham, had finished, the older man rushed forward to embrace him. Like most teenage sons, the younger Winn was pleased but a little embarrassed. Walking back to his post the older man brushed away his tears. And now once more, though for very different reasons Winn was a man with a lean, strained look on his face.

He turned his back on the straight. This was the terrible moment so many in the crowd had been waiting for and there were calls of: "Shame!" Sometimes there is no one in sight when the gun goes off, and the climax of a long day is a little empty. With one minute to go on an already darkening field now lit by arc lamps, there were no runners who had recently come in through the back of the Collegian Harriers ground—until suddenly a growing tidal wave of yells and cheers swept in from the far side of the soccer pitch. The boos pelted Winn but he stood his ground, feet planted slightly apart, the creases in his khaki trousers still immaculate and his blue blazer neatly buttoned in the middle over his Comrades tie.

Mick Winn prepares to signal the end
of the 1979 Comrades time limit;
a runner vainly sprints toward the finish.

The roaring grew to a pitch equal to the announcer's increasingly frenzied delivery. The crowd was on its feet. Among those of us near the finish, it was impossible to see who was coming. The crowd had just begun its final choral chant in unison, as the last 10 seconds ticked away, when the lumbering, portly figure of a white-haired old gent hove into view, flanked on each side by a handler. Like a bewildered tug battling a choppy sea, he rumbled forward, probably a little dazed by the commotion and his own fatigue, as Winn's gun arm straightened itself over his head and his face peered intently down at the stopwatch face. Clearly Winn would fire as humanly close to the instant as possible.

"I cannot let myself be swayed one way or the other," Winn had said earlier. "People blame me for shooting the gun, but you have to have some kind of limit to it, don't you? Otherwise when can you say the race is over? No, I don't like doing it, in a way, and I keep my back to the straight so I have no possibility of being influenced."

I hadn't considered the old tradition anything more than a rather amusing touch to keep the crowd there to the finish, but suddenly I found myself yelling, raising my voice in the overall bedlam, shouting to the old fellow to hurry up, for God's sake. It hardly seemed possible that he could get any closer and not make it in time. He even seemed to rally slightly at the very close, and his last steps had a definite kind of lilt as he came right up within touching range of Mick Winn's back. Then the gun smoked and the shot exploded—a mere instant before he crossed the finish line.

There was a general loud wail of disappointment. It was sad and yet just. Without limits, boundaries, or definition, there is no sense to any of it.

About the Author

JAMES E. SHAPIRO is a freelance writer whose work has appeared in many magazines and newspapers for the past ten years. He is also a gourmet chef who has worked in various New York restaurants. Author of one previous book, *On the Road— The Marathon,* he is a Harvard graduate, has served in the Peace Corps and has been running races, marathons and ultramarathons for six years. He now lives in Manhattan and runs 15 miles a day.

Milton Keynes UK
Ingram Content Group UK Ltd.
UKHW02071805 0424
440683UK00013B/370